SIGNS
of
LOVE

SIGNS

of

LOVE

Christian Liturgy in the
Everyday Life of the Family

Msgr. Renzo Bonetti

Printed in the United States of America

Cover illustration: The Marriage Icon *courtesy of Mistero Grande Foundation, used with permission.*
Cover and page design by Strange Last Name
Page layout by PerfecType, Nashville, Tennessee

Bonetti, Renzo.
    Signs of love : Christian liturgy in the everyday life of the family / Renzo Bonetti ; translated
by Brent Orrell and Alessandro Sona. – Frankin, Tennessee : Seedbed Publishing, ©2017.

        x, 146 pages ; 21 cm.

        Includes bibliographical references (pages 139-146)
        Translation of: La liturgia della famiglia : la coppia sacramento dell'amore
        ISBN 9781628244427 (paperback)
        ISBN 9781628244434 (Mobi)
        ISBN 9781628244441 (ePub)
        ISBN 9781628244458 (uPDF)

        "Through the iconography of ordinary marriages, Bonetti shows us how married love,
        the "great mystery" St. Paul writes about in Ephesians 5, can make us present to the
        very heart of the church itself. To understand the Trinity, he says, we should look to
        the lives of Christian couples as they reenact Jesus' self-sacrifice at Calvary. Through
        its powerful examination of church sacraments – baptism, confirmation, forgiveness,
        Eucharistic union, and last rites – Signs of love shows us that these "outward, visible
        signs of inward visible grace" are not just for Sunday but, when incarnated in the life
        of the married couple, vital tools for discipleship and evangelization."—Publisher.

        1. Married people--Religious life. 2. Liturgics. 3. Sacraments. 4. Christian life--
        Catholic authors. 5. Spiritual formation. 6. Spiritual exercises. I. Title. II. La liturgia
        della famiglia : la coppia sacramento dell'amore. English.

BV4596.M3 B6616 2017   248.8   2017950157

SEEDBED PUBLISHING
Franklin, Tennessee
seedbed.com

CONTENTS

FOREWORD

Signs of Love is a translation of a book by Monsignor Renzo Bonetti, a Roman Catholic priest who lives near Verona in northern Italy. Originally published as *The Liturgy of the Family*, *Signs of Love* is an extended meditation on marriage as a living icon of God's love. In Bonetti's words, each marriage is "a book of God written in flesh" that instructs the couple and the world in the relationship of total self-giving that exists between the three Persons of the Trinity: Father, Son, and Holy Spirit. To see Jesus is to see the Father. To see a married couple is to be given a glimpse of the Trinitarian love that powers all existence and to be present to the very heart of the church itself.

Since 2012, Truro Anglican Church in Fairfax, Virginia (www. truroanglican.com), has partnered with Bonetti and the organization he leads, Mistero Grande (The Great Mystery, http:// www.misterogrande.org/), to deepen our understanding of this teaching. We have learned that Bonetti's work is, above all, a theology of relationship. God, through his Son, is intimately connected to and identified with humanity. He entrusted Jesus to an earthly father and mother who cared for him as he grew up within an extended community of family and neighbors. In his teaching, Jesus expanded the scope of the family ("Who is my mother, and who are my brothers?" [Matt. 12:46–50 ESV]) to include his disciples and intimate friends. It is through this radical expansion of our concept of the family that Truro is learning how our own families can become, in don Renzo's words, the "Trinitarian greenhouses" in which new faith is seeded, nurtured, and grown.

There are many how-to books for improving marriage. *Signs of Love* is not one of them. Rather, it is meditation to help Christians—single, married, divorced, widowed—explore God's purposes in creating the physical, emotional, psychological, and spiritual pairing of male and female in a lifelong bond. In short, it is not a book about how to fix a marriage but rather how marriage can begin to fix us. At Truro, we are persuaded that the "profound mystery" St. Paul teaches in Ephesians 5 is a much grander and more serious and beautiful thing than we ever suspected. It is, quite literally, a primary means by which we share in the Father's work to redeem and renew his creation. In this way, the sort of self-giving love embodied in the apostle Paul's writing is inherently evangelical.

Monsignor Bonetti, or don Renzo as he is known to us, is fond of saying that the church without an evangelism strategy is nothing more than an ideology. And in a day and age where growing numbers of people have little or no Christian experience, the fact that the great mystery of marriage provides such a strategy is good news. In a changing culture, it is the family who stands on the frontier of evangelization. It is the family who reaches out as a living demonstration of the love of God to those who most often feel far from God. It is the family who mentors the young adult, who takes in the foster child, and the family who can reclaim the idea of the domestic church.

Early in my ministry, I was introduced to the writings of the polish priest Karol Wojtyla, the man who later became Pope John Paul II. His work, particularly his *Theology of the Body*, introduced me to a fuller understanding of Christ the Bridegroom who pursues his people—his bride. Scripture begins with a wedding in a garden. It likewise ends with a wedding in a garden. The middle of the Bible (Song of Songs) is a nuptial song—the soundtrack of Scripture. And, of course, Jesus performs his first miracle at a wedding in Cana of Galilee before entering Samaria to woo the woman at the well (a nuptial-type scene). The language of marriage is so prominent in Scripture that the whole of the Christian life must somehow be shaped by the great mystery. God first loved us—indeed, pursued and wooed us. Everything else stems from that first love.

It wasn't until I was introduced to Bonetti's work that I began seeing how I could lead our parish into living the theology of the body. *Signs of Love* shows how the sacraments of the faith offer a rhythm for family life. Some of us reading this book will be familiar with these sacraments and their purpose in the history of the Christian faith. Others will be introduced to the sacraments for the first time. Thus, a word of explanation is in order.

A *sacrament* is an outward and visible sign of an inward, invisible grace. And there is scriptural evidence that each of the seven were witnessed or practiced by Jesus. While the Protestant Reformers elevated baptism and Communion above the others with the Radical Reformers adding foot-washing to the list, each of these sacraments is practiced in some way by every stream of the Christian tradition. Each stream practices the Eucharist, Lord's Supper, or Holy Communion. Each stream also practices baptism. For streams of the Christian tradition who practice "believer baptism," the baptism itself serves as a confirmation of the believer's faith in Christ. Similarly, the acts of marriage, forgiveness, anointing of the sick, and the Word all have a prominent place in each stream of the Christian tradition, though understood or prized differently.

I've spent much of my life and ministry engaged in the work of reconciliation and peacemaking; and before something can be mended, we must first acknowledge a state of brokenness. In the broken places is where God's grace often shines the brightest. It is without question that much of the church today is in need of mending. It should be no secret that much of the brokenness in the church is a direct result of the brokenness in the little domestic churches that make up the whole. Whole neighborhoods and communities are broken because the role of the family as the front line of the church's witness is missing.

But in Christ, there is always reason for hope. The reasons for the church's decline are what inspire hope. The body of Christ becomes strong in the broken place when domestic church is recovered as essential to the ecclesial church. The church recovers a way of life so that the pattern of our lives in Christ, sacramentally marked, becomes a means of grace to all who are touched by our people. Christianity ceases to be ideology and becomes life.

Publishing a work of this sort is only possible because of some very special early adopters. Brent Orrell from our parish and Alessandro Sona with Mistero Grande did the painstaking work of translation. Brent was the first to pilot a study group of the book in our parish. Brent's vision for the book is that it is best read and digested in community. To that end, Aaron Williams—a PhD student at the John Paul II Institute for Studies on Marriage and Family at Catholic University in Washington, DC, and a member of our parish—wrote the study guide for each chapter of the book with the aim of provoking discussion and action. Chaney Mullins, Hannah King, and Matthew Hemsley on our staff were early champions of the book and component parts of our project as our parish learns to love as God loves. Chris Backert and Gannon Sims with Fresh Expressions US caught the vision of domestic church as key to the re-evangelization of North America. This book is but a facet of a growing project that we hope will contribute in some way to that end.

We share it with you in excitement and gratitude!

—Reverend Dr. Tory Baucum
Rector, Truro Anglican Church
Fairfax, Virginia

THE LITURGY OF THE CHURCH

and

THE LITURGY OF THE FAMILY

THE LITURGY OF THE CHURCH

This book is a meditation on and prayer for the great mystery that spouses receive through the sacrament of marriage (see Ephesians 5:32). For marriage is more than the wedding ceremony itself. It is a mystery that endures throughout the life of the couple, a mystery that has its own liturgy and rites.

In this first chapter, we wish to rediscover the beauty of what the church celebrates and lives through the liturgy of the church and how the family—the little, or domestic, church—echoes, extends, and points us back to the church's larger liturgy.

We need to begin by deepening our understanding of *liturgy* as something far more than the religious ceremonies of the church. To go deeper we must focus on the Person at the heart of liturgy, Jesus Christ.

The *Catechism of the Catholic Church* teaches the centrality of Jesus this way: Christ is always present in his church, especially in her liturgical celebrations.[1] And again:

> Seated at the right hand of the Father and pouring out the Holy Spirit on his body, which is the church, Christ now acts through the sacraments he instituted to communicate his grace . . . By the action of Christ and the power of the Holy Spirit they make present efficaciously the grace that they signify.[2]

Jesus acts through the church, but his actions are not entrusted to the goodwill or skill of people. Instead, his powerful action within the church is founded on the apostles' mandate. As the *Catechism* teaches:

> Just as Christ was sent by the Father so also he sent the apostles, filled with the Holy Spirit . . . so that the work of salvation which they preached should be set in train through the sacrifice and sacraments, around which the entire liturgical life revolves.[3]

Further on, it presents the other side of the liturgy:

> Christ, indeed, always associates the Church with himself in [the liturgy] in which God is perfectly glorified and men are sanctified. The Church is his beloved Bride who calls to her Lord and through him offers worship to the eternal Father.[4]

Every church liturgy, then, has two dimensions: first, an *ascending* dimension, in which we give glory to God—Father, Son, and Holy Spirit—to praise, bless, and thank the Lord; second, a *descending* dimension, in which the Lord comes to meet us, sanctify us, and help us grow in his life.

We must emphasize that the *whole* church is involved in this action of praise, and the *whole* church benefits from the salvation that comes from the Father through the Son in the Holy

Spirit in *every* liturgical celebration. Even a small congregation—a few people, celebrating a single baptism—is joined by the whole church. When a single priest prays the Liturgy of the Hours, he celebrates with the church, and the church with him. In this way, the Christian is never alone. Through the Holy Spirit, we are all always part of one body that is the church.

During these liturgical unions, the Holy Spirit makes Jesus and the mystery of his love real, creating and sustaining the link between Jesus and each one of us. In the church, the Spirit forms and makes visible the body of Jesus. The *Catechism* expresses the mystery of Jesus' love, shown in the church's liturgy:

> Christian liturgy not only recalls the events that saved us but actualizes them, makes them present. The Paschal mystery of Christ is celebrated, not repeated. It is the celebrations that are repeated, and in each celebration there is an outpouring of the Holy Spirit that makes the unique mystery present.[5]

The paschal mystery of Christ, the center of Christian life and faith, is beyond time and eternal. While it cannot be repeated, the liturgy makes it present to us. As the *Catechism* tells us, "The whole liturgical life of the church revolves around the Eucharistic sacrifice and the sacraments."[6] It further explains, "The sacraments are efficacious signs of grace, instituted by Christ and entrusted to the Church."[7]

Through the liturgy, the mysteries lived by Jesus—his passion, death, and resurrection—are present to us. Entering the "eternal now" through the liturgy, we go to meet the living Jesus. The living Jesus we meet in the liturgy is the same for us now as he was for those Christians living in AD 1400. This same Jesus will meet his people in the liturgy when Christians gather a hundred years from now. Jesus is always present in the mystery of his salvation through the rites that join us to him. He saves us and joins us, the church, to himself to give praise to the Father.

THE LITURGY OF THE FAMILY: THE LITTLE CHURCH

We now turn to the liturgy as it is expressed in the life of the family. We call the family the *little* or *domestic* church. The domestic church has its own liturgy that echoes and points to the universal church.

In *Familiaris Consortio*, Saint John Paul II writes:

> Christian marriage, like the other sacraments, "whose purpose is to sanctify people, to build up the body of Christ, and finally, to give worship to God" (*Sacrosanctum Concilium,* 59) is in itself a liturgical action glorifying God in Jesus Christ and in the Church.[8]

For most, the idea that a married couple's everyday life forms a unique liturgy is surprising, but its importance cannot be overstated. This small liturgy is joined to the great liturgy of the church and has within itself a distinct ministry and liturgical task.

The liturgical–ritual dimension of this spousal liturgy is in danger of being completely forgotten, because those charged with pastoral care frequently feel overwhelmed by problems that appear more urgent than the needs of the family. Modern pastoral culture looks to the rite of marriage itself in the hope that it is sufficient to sustain and equip the couple for the rest of their lives. This is a flawed and incomplete understanding of the spousal liturgy.

SPOUSES: LITURGICAL MINISTERS OF THE MARRIAGE RITE

In celebrating the marriage rite, the spouses, not the priest, are ministers of the liturgy. The priest is the church's witness; he blesses the spouses. But the man and the woman are really the liturgical ministers of the marriage rite.

In the spousal liturgy, the first liturgical act is the rite of the sacrament of marriage, where God joins husband and wife in a one-flesh union. The spouses are ministers of the sacrament, by means of, and with the power of, their baptismal priesthood, the priesthood of all believers.[9]

The two baptized persons who marry already belong to Jesus, the central actor in the marriage rite who is acting in and with the church's liturgy. It is Jesus who gives the spouses to each other through their exchange of consent and through the pouring forth of the Holy Spirit.

In the celebration of the marriage sacrament, the spouses occupy the place that a priest does when he celebrates the Mass or hears confession. Spouses make Jesus present, and Jesus gives them to one another. As they exchange vows, they lend their voices so that Jesus can say to each of them, "Yes, I give you to one another."

In every sacrament, it is always Jesus who acts. It is Jesus who baptizes. It is Jesus who gives the Holy Spirit in confirmation. The priest and the bishop are signs, but it is not the priest who baptizes; it is not the bishop who confirms. It is Jesus who baptizes and confirms through the priest or the bishop. In the Mass, it is Jesus who celebrates. "This is my body," he says, using the voice of the priest. In penance, it is Jesus who absolves; in anointing the sick, it is Jesus who gives comfort and healing. And in holy orders and matrimony, it is Jesus who joins the spouses in a one-flesh union. Thus, when we fail to recognize the spouses as the ministers of the marriage sacrament, we distort its meaning and diminish its importance.

As the priest acts in the name of Jesus when he celebrates the Mass, so spouses act in the name of Jesus when they minister in the sacrament of marriage. Of course, couples prepare for marriage; they discern and choose whether one is made for the other. But in the final analysis, it is Jesus who brings and joins the two baptized Christians together.

Earlier we established that every sacrament has an ascending and a descending dimension. The nuptial liturgy *ascends,* giving glory, praise, and worship to the Trinity, praising and blessing God for the creation of man and woman made in his image and likeness. The four blessings of the marriage rite invoke the Holy Spirit upon the spouses and begin with a prayer of praise and thanksgiving to the Lord for the great gift of having created man and woman. These blessings make clear that the marriage rite is an act of liturgical worship, of entering into the eternal now of Christ and his church. The nuptial liturgy also *descends.* In the descending dimension, the Lord empowers the spouses to be able to live out the love of Christ in their life together.

Familiaris Consortio underlines these fundamental truths:

> The Spirit which the Lord pours forth gives a new heart, and renders man and woman capable of loving one another as Christ has loved us. . . . [The spouses] are called to live the very charity of Christ who gave Himself on the Cross.[10]

Spouses must do more than celebrate the rite of the marriage. They are called to live the love that gave itself on the cross!

In the coming chapters, we will continue to explore the characteristics that all the sacraments share with the marriage sacrament. For instance, as a priest celebrates the continuity of Christ's donation in the Eucharist, so spouses celebrate a continuity of Christ's sacrificial love through their married life.

Every marriage is a new *yes* of God ("Yes, I have done a beautiful thing") to the creative action of man and woman, who are made in God's image and likeness.[11] Every marriage mirrors and repeats the same *yes* present in the creation of the first man and woman. Every marriage is also a new *yes* to the covenant of love between the Creator and humanity, between Christ and the church, so that this love may continue to live and communicate itself through a new couple. God wants to extend and grow this loving covenant between Christ and the church; he does so by asking the spouses to continuously share and celebrate it.

The celebration of marriage is a new expression of God's love for humanity. Through marriage, he redeems, saves, and renews love from all the decay that may afflict it. Regardless of whether the couple is Christian, marriage provides a common grace that tells of God's "in the beginning" blessing of creation. In the sacrament of marriage Jesus appropriates the marriage and makes it an effective sign of grace for the glory of God.

SPOUSES CONTINUE THE LITURGY OF MARRIAGE IN THEIR LIFE TOGETHER

Familiaris Consortio tells us, "Marriage is in itself a liturgical action glorifying God in Jesus Christ and in the Church."[12] This underlines the continuity between the marriage rite and the spouses' lives. This continuity can also be found in *The Rite of Marriage*: "The true practice of conjugal love, and the whole meaning of the family life which results from it, have this aim: that the couple be ready with stout hearts to cooperate with the love of the Creator and the Savior."[13]

The rite speaks of a "true practice," which must continue throughout married life. Spouses are called to continue, to remember, to actualize the mystery of Christ's passion, death, and resurrection as well as the nuptial mystery of Christ with the church.

The Rite of Marriage explicitly affirms this concept with these wonderful words:

> God, who has called the spouses *to* the marriage, continues to call them *in* the marriage. Those who get married in Christ, by means of the faith in the Word of God, are made capable to fruitfully celebrate, to live in holiness and to publicly witness the mystery of the union of Christ and the Church.[14]

The passage speaks about a lifelong fruitful celebration of the mystery of the union of Christ and the church. The fruitful celebration discussed above is not found only in a rite of the church but in the entire life of the couple. In the domestic context, the celebration of marriage is meant to describe both worship (ascending liturgy) and the sanctification God accomplishes in those who engage in it (descending liturgy). This concept of the ongoing celebration of the marriage sacrament emphasizes the beauty, power, and meaning of the fruitful celebration of the mystery of the union of Christ and the church within the domestic church.

One of the most famous liturgical scholars of the post-Vatican II era, Achille M. Triacca, studied the original Latin of the Council text and deepens our understanding of the liturgy of the family for married couples:

> Every "liturgy of the conjugal life" is directly related to the vitality of the [church's] liturgy. If this were not the case, the conjugal ministry would be in vain as well as the dynamisms coming from the fact that spouses are ministers of a permanent sacrament.[15]

The passage explains clearly the concept of *permanent sacrament.* If a sacrament is permanent, then there is a permanent ministry for those who receive and engage in it. Marriage is a permanent sacrament, since spouses do not merely *celebrate* the sacrament of marriage; spouses *are* the sacrament of marriage—in the same way that bread and wine, blessed by God through the priest, is the Eucharist.

Thus, in carrying out their *yes* and their mutual promise of sacrificial love and fidelity in their married, or *conjugal,* life, the rite celebrated in the church in the beginning (*in fieri*) is connected to the conjugal life (*in facto*). In this way, marriage becomes a true liturgy of life, linking the great liturgy of the church to the domestic life of the couple, expressed in family and surrounding community. This liturgy of marriage—operating through Jesus within the spouses—is for the glory of God, the sanctification of the couple, and the salvation of the world.

Familiaris Consortio tells us:

> Their belonging to each other is the real representation, by means of the sacramental sign, of the very relationship of Christ with the Church. Spouses are therefore the permanent reminder to

the Church of what happened on the Cross . . . Of this salvation
event, marriage, like every sacrament, is a memorial, actuation
and prophecy.[16]

The domestic liturgy is signified by ordinary signs a couple
exhibits in day-to-day life, rather than formal signs celebrated
in the rites of the church. The priest celebrates the mystery of
the cross in an extraordinary way through the Eucharist. The
spouses celebrate the same mystery in mutual self-donation.
They celebrate the mystery of Christ's love in their life through
gestures that form a unique spousal liturgy—an embrace after
being apart during the day or a kiss. Through the love of the
spouses, Christ loves and continues to donate himself to them,
their children and family, and the community of relationships
in which they are embedded.

In living the sacrament of marriage, spouses discover the source
of love and spiritual energy required to transform every instant
of their life into a domestic liturgy. This goes well beyond the
clerical understanding of liturgy as ritual: domestic liturgy is
not ritual, but the love of God expressed through the normal
activities of everyday life.

In this domestic liturgy, the whole life of a married couple
becomes a *sign* of Jesus' presence as husband and wife pass
from, "I do this because it is what we have become used to or
because it is expected," to, "I do this because we are united in
the name of the Lord." Through marriage, spouses are called
and enabled to assume a ministry in both church and society
that expresses—within and through conjugal life—praise, glory,
and thanks to the Lord while helping the family and community
to grow in holiness.

The more we praise the Lord, the more the Lord sanctifies
us. All married life can be considered an everlasting liturgy of
praise to the Lord and an ongoing act of sanctification. Nothing
is discarded with the exception of sin, which is always a betrayal
of marriage.

The words of Saint Robert Bellarmine further strengthen this concept of the continuous liturgy of marriage:

> The sacrament of marriage can be considered in two ways: the first when it is celebrated, the second while it endures. It is in fact a sacrament similar to the Eucharist, which is a sacrament not only while it is celebrated, but also while it endures, because while the spouses live their union, it is always the sacrament of Christ and the Church.[17]

Marriage is an active, dynamic, living sacrament, a union of two free persons, who in every moment choose between doing and not doing, saying and not saying, embracing and not embracing. The love that empowers each to choose the good of the other incarnates the love of Christ for the church.

The Ecclesial Dimension

The liturgy of the church expresses the worship that the whole community of God, together with the Lord Jesus, raises up to the Father. As we noted earlier, the Christian is never alone in the liturgy, for it is always an act of *all* the church. The liturgy is an ecclesial event owned by no individual but lived in profound and mutual communion in the Holy Spirit. For this reason, there is a unique liturgical celebration, which belongs to all the church's members, gathered around the resurrected Lord.

In the home setting, the sacrament of marriage is expressed in its own unique way. A Christian marriage is not a fragment of the ecclesial mosaic, but rather the church itself, at the very core of the nuptial covenant with Christ the Bridegroom. A married couple does not merely mimic or foreshadow the church. Rather, marriage *makes present* the heart of the church itself. The liturgical action of marriage, like all liturgical actions, can never be isolated. Rather, it always lives and celebrates in communion with the whole church.

The Christian couple is a unique and specific domestic expression of the church itself. The faith experiences lived at home have a liturgical character. At the same time, the domestic liturgy must always be linked to the larger liturgy of the church and the Christian community so that it can be authenticated and celebrated in its fullness. Otherwise, it is reduced from liturgy to private devotion. In its communion with the larger church, the domestic liturgy becomes truly liturgical and permits domestic acts to be manifested and proclaimed.

To be effective and sustained, the family and its liturgy must also take part in the sacramental celebrations that the domestic church does not have, and cannot give to, itself. Above all, the family must participate in the Sunday Eucharist to be drawn into the larger family of the church. In this way, it shows itself to be part of the church, from which it receives baptism, confirmation, Eucharist, and penance. The family is always a point of interest and love for the church; it must be connected to the church's liturgical pathway, and to the timing and rhythm of the church's liturgical year. In this way, the domestic liturgy is authenticated and located within the ecclesial dimension of the whole community of God rather than operating in isolation.

The Christological Dimension

In all liturgical actions, Jesus Christ makes himself present with the mystery of his death and resurrection. Through these actions, he extends the history of salvation in the temporal realm. His sacramental presence extends beyond such simple signs and gestures as pouring water on the head for a baptism, breaking bread for the Eucharist, or giving a sign of peace for reconciliation.

The permanence of the marriage sacrament implies a continuous outpouring of the presence of Jesus in the family. Thus, in the life of a married couple there is not only a marriage ceremony—an outward recall of God's covenant—but an active participation of Jesus through personal and living signs.

The living liturgy of the family means that Jesus is always present in our homes. We must always be aware of the mystery of Christ's presence! Again, the analogy to the Eucharist is necessary and fitting. If a priest celebrates the Mass without thinking about the fact that it is Jesus who is acting through him, he would be an automaton, a man who has memorized the words of the rite without those words having real and immediate meaning. Such a priest wouldn't be in the right condition to help others perceive the presence of the mystery. The more the priest recognizes that he is the sacrament of Jesus, that Jesus is enacting the Mass through him, the more he understands the mystery of the sacrament and the mystery of his own relationship to Jesus. This priest, operating with deep knowledge of his words and actions, is better able to communicate the real presence of Christ to those he serves.

It is the same for spouses. The more they are aware of the sacramental nature of their marriage, the more alive they are to the presence of Jesus in their home, the more Jesus resides with them in their home. Every act, every gesture, every person who enters their home is incorporated into the liturgy of their life, which brings greater and greater praise and glory to the Lord. Conversely, if the spouses live their lives forgetting the sacrament of marriage, then their conjugal life cannot become a place of sanctification. Many spouses live together for years without caring about their liturgy with God. They fill the space intended for Jesus with the liturgy of holidays, or the liturgy of entertainment, or the liturgy of consumption. The spouses are asleep to the mystery of the conjugal sacrament, a mystery as profound and as important as the sacrament of Christ's priesthood.

In *Gaudium et Spes* we read:

> The Savior of men and the Spouse of the Church comes into the lives of married Christians through the sacrament of matrimony. He abides with them thereafter so that just as He loved the Church and handed Himself over on her behalf, the spouses may love each other with perpetual fidelity through mutual self-bestowal.[18]

"He abides with them," but why? Because he donated himself. In the same way, the spouses are called to donate themselves to each other to celebrate the love of Christ for the church. Jesus wants to continue to celebrate his total donation in the life of every married couple. He wants to continue to celebrate the reality of the body given for life, even up to dying. Christ has a great desire to celebrate this self-donation in, with, and through the couple!

This original presence of Christ in the life of Christian spouses operates in three dimensions. First, marriage is a *distinctive sign* of the domestic church, an active support in the evangelization of their children and the world, and at the center of the church's worship. Second, the resurrected Lord works through the family to praise, thank, and bless the Father through the sanctification of the couple, whom he has called to incarnate his spousal love for the church. This particular presence of the Lord harmonizes with the spousal union in all its different expressions. Finally, common prayer and other gestures of faith assume a liturgical character as acts of worship to Jesus Christ, who identifies himself with the married couple to give glory to the Father.

These concepts feel very high and abstract but are, in fact, very practical. It is as if Jesus takes the two spouses under his arm and says, "Come with me to praise the Father. Your marriage is a beautiful thing and we will praise the Father for the love that is singing in you. We will bless the Father who created you, male and female in his image, and we will bless his Son who will renew, purify, and sanctify you in and through your marriage." It is Christ himself who helps the spouses in giving praise and glory to the Father, as is done in the celebration of the Eucharist: "By him, and with him, and in him, in the unity of the Holy Spirit, all glory and honor are yours, almighty Father God."

HOW SPOUSES PRACTICE LITURGICAL SERVICE

Achille M. Triacca explains that, "The liturgy of the conjugal life makes visible the invisible presence of the Holy Spirit and the love experienced within the Trinity . . . as well as the Christ's love for his church."[19]

In this *ministry of visibility*, the spouses are called to make visible the love of God. Only the spouses, in their conjugal life of reciprocal love, are able to say to the world that God is love; only they can make visible the nature of the love exchanged among Father, Son, and Holy Spirit.

The priest has the ministry of preaching the Word; the spouses have the ministry of visibility. What the priest says through words, spouses are called to say in the flesh. The priest explains a book made of paper; the spouses are a book made of flesh. With this book, one doesn't need to know how to read, but only to see, because the spouses participate in Christ's love for his church and are a reflection of Trinitarian life. Triacca affirms this incarnational reality: "The 'great gift' given to the spouses actualizes itself in the 'domestic liturgy' by means of gestures and words."[20]

But *what* does the domestic church celebrate? Or, better, *who* celebrates? In *Evangelization and Sacrament of Marriage*, we read:

> In the sacramental encounter, Jesus Christ gives the spouses a new way of being, through which they are conformed to his image, the bridegroom of the church, and taken into a particular state of being within the community of God.[21]

It is, therefore, Jesus Christ himself who celebrates in and with the spouses. It is Jesus who makes real his life in and with them. Through them, we see his donation of himself to us. The spouses enact the glorification and sanctification of Jesus in the strength of the Holy Spirit, celebrating the mysteries of Jesus' love in themselves. We will now try to identify these mysteries, so that we can see how spouses celebrate domestically what is celebrated in the church.

In the church we celebrate the feasts of the Annunciation, of Christmas, and of the Presentation of Christ. We celebrate his life in Nazareth and, during Holy Week, his passion, death, and resurrection. During Pentecost, we celebrate the descent of the Holy Spirit. But how are these mysteries celebrated in the family?

In the domestic liturgy, spouses remember and continue Christ's incarnation in a special way. Through small gestures and words of love, the spouses make real the love of God for humanity. The Word of God has communicated to the spouses his love for humanity and for the church.

Holy Scripture provides us with a guide for understanding the liturgy in the family in the same way it helps us understand the liturgy of the church. By reading, searching, and understanding Scripture, spouses learn about the incarnation: the Word of God was made flesh as an expression of Jesus' love for humanity and the church. This incarnation is not something that happened only in the past. It is an action that happens even now, through the spouses, who are called both to remember and actualize it. To illustrate: Jesus hears the shout of a blind man from afar, "Son of David, have pity on me!" He hears and heals the woman who touches the hem of his cloak (see Luke 18:38; 8:43–48).

Jesus lowered himself to be among us. How can the spouses celebrate and replicate the lowering and bowing down of Jesus? Spouses can bow down before each other, each taking onto themselves the faults of the other. Spouses can agree to share their blessings and problems, to be *one* as Christ makes himself one with the church, as the Word of God makes himself one with humanity. This unity can be practiced in every aspect of their common life—from tender embracing, to the unity of their bodies, to the attention paid to each other, to the service rendered to each other or to their children.

All of these are gestures of unity, and each is a celebration, a rite, which incarnates the love of God. The smallest acts—the welcoming home and the being welcomed, offering refreshment, sharing the day's events, and simple listening to the details of each other's lives—all are gestures that celebrate both the love of God, which desires to be united with human flesh, and of Christ's unity with the church.

The unitive dimension of the marriage sacrament extends beyond the couple and the family. This love is also intended to celebrate unity outside itself. If a couple visits someone in need or cares for a sick person or for a child, they express the love of the Word of God for humanity and the love of Christ for the church.

With this understanding, we can also see how teaching catechism, serving the parish, or providing help to people is a bowing of the couple toward others, a unitive reality celebrated outside the home. The family is called to celebrate these mysteries, this domestic liturgy, in service to the world. This liturgy has its heart in the home, but it is not for the home alone. It is meant to be celebrated for and in the world.

When we are aware of being a sacrament of Jesus, all of life becomes more precious. Each moment is made sacramental, filled with extraordinary meaning. In the life of a couple and family, the Word has been fully incarnated; he has been excluded from nothing, and nothing in the conjugal life is excluded from this re-expression of his incarnation.

The life of Jesus in Nazareth gives us a very clear example of how simple gestures can become praise, glory, and sanctification. It is the whole life of Jesus that saves us and not just the passion. The small acts of daily life, like those shared by Jesus and his family in Nazareth, make up the domestic liturgy of the couple.

These acts of worshipful praise help to sanctify us and lead us to the celebration of the passion, death, and resurrection. Spouses reenact the liturgy of sacrifice in themselves. Think of a spouse waking early in the morning to work on behalf of his wife and children, or a spouse who stays at home to care with loving kindness for the children. These are costly, beautiful sacrifices for the well-being of the spouses and the family.

This liturgy of sacrifice extends and expresses the love and sacrifice of Jesus, allowing him to continue to celebrate his saving work in the lives of spouses and families. Giving the body for love is much more than a sexual relationship. It is a total gift, a matter of how spouses live twenty-four hours a day the liturgy of mutual self-donation.

Chapter 2

BAPTISM
and
THE LITURGY OF THE FAMILY

CONTINUITY OF THE NUPTIAL
LITURGICAL ACT

The nuptial liturgy does not end with the wedding service, "The Mass is ended, go in peace." Rather, the nuptial liturgy continues as it is celebrated each day in the life of the spouses. Saint Robert Bellarmine shows us how the sacrament of marriage expresses itself:

> The sacrament of marriage can be considered in two ways: the first when it is celebrated, the second while it endures after the celebration. It in fact is a sacrament similar to the Eucharist, which is sacrament not only when it is accomplished, but also while it endures: because, as long as the spouses live, their union is always a sacrament of Christ and of the Church.[1]

In the previous chapter, we saw the two dimensions of liturgy: giving glory to the Father (ascending) and the sanctification of people by God (descending). In the ongoing sacrament of marriage, sanctification comes to the spouses.

With the nuptial blessing, the spouses, consecrated in the fire of the Holy Spirit, are no longer only two baptized persons, but also one flesh. This union enables them to express their baptismal identity in a new way, with a new effect.[2] A new liturgical expression begins. Before, the single person lived his baptismal priesthood, now the two married spouses become one flesh. The priestly character of the baptized is carried out in and through their one-flesh union.

For this reason, we can say that the liturgical-ritual act accomplished with the rite of the marriage is expressed on an ongoing basis as a mission that spouses are called to celebrate. In married life, the spouses have many tasks, including rearing children or serving the church or society. But for Christian spouses there is also a liturgical mandate to worship and give praise to God, and to be sanctified by him.

The spouses, made one with Jesus the Bridegroom, continue his mission of praise to the Father for their mutual sanctification and their mission to bless and sanctify others they encounter. The Jesus who is in them is both the Son who praises the Father and he who worked as a carpenter beside Joseph. This Jesus bestows salvation, and the spouses actualize him in their own particular way.

With the grace of the sacrament of marriage, the spouses place themselves within the priestly community, the whole community of baptized people, with a new priestly mission. The presence of Jesus with them, in the unity of their marriage, permanently enables them to live a two-fold domestic liturgy, giving glory to God and welcoming the sanctification that comes from the Father. In *Familiaris Consortio* we read:

> Christian spouses profess their gratitude to God for the sublime gift bestowed on them of being able to live in their married and family lives the very love of God for people and that of the Lord Jesus for the Church, His bride . . . so the same sacrament

confers on them the grace and moral obligation of transforming their whole lives into a "spiritual sacrifice" (cf. 1 Peter 2:5; *Lumen gentium*, 34).[3]

This spiritual sacrifice allows us to connect the Mass, celebrated in the church, with the life of the spouses celebrated in the home.

With the grace of the marriage, the two spouses are called to celebrate in their relationship the love between Jesus and the church. This is a liturgical mission, in which their baptismal priesthood becomes a domestic church within the one-flesh union.

As time passes, all the ordinary activities of life become a liturgy of praise and sanctification. We must look at this liturgy from the point of view of ordinariness, and in the light of Jesus who is with and in the spouses.

The liturgy of the spouses is the liturgy of Bethlehem, which from the outside appears to be poor and full of the needs of a child. Yet in the midst of poverty and need there is Jesus, God in the image of man! In the liturgy of Bethlehem, in the simplicity of a child who must be brought to maturity, the couple relives this liturgy. In the liturgy of Nazareth, the wonder of the beginning—the annunciation, the extraordinary birth, the shepherds, the wise men—gives way to normality, to the everyday repetition of gestures that obscure the beauty of the Holy Child's birth. The work of the carpenter seems to also plane away the sentiment of wonder. Mary and Joseph see this young man as he grows. Mary knows that he is the Son of God, but the passage of time and the absence of new miracles seem to cancel the prophecy. She forgets the words of the prophets: "He will be the Savior"; "He will be the Messiah." In Nazareth the highest celebration of normality arises.

Suddenly, in manhood, Jesus begins the liturgy of public life by "standing up in public." His words and deeds divide the people into friends and enemies. In declaring himself the Son of God, he is considered a madman and a blasphemer. Others say, "Who does he think he is? He is the son of the carpenter!" His miracles and great signs unleash envy and fear.

In the end, the liturgies of Bethlehem and Nazareth give way to the liturgy of pain and loneliness. The world needs the pain and tears that the family experiences. It is part of the total gift, part of gradually but consciously learning to lose all. If we give everything, death can steal nothing from us! ("I have power to lay it down, and power to take it up again," said Jesus [John 10:18].) It is the final embrace through which all those who were not united to Jesus in the flesh have been united to him by sharing the cup of pain and death. This is the weekday liturgy that spouses are called to celebrate with solemnity.

SPOUSES CONTINUE BAPTISMAL LITURGY IN THEIR CHILDREN AND COMMUNITY

The continuation of the baptismal liturgy includes not only children, if the couple has them, but everyone they meet. A married couple can have a thousand children. They have as many children as they encounter along life's path, because the couple, father and mother, is able to recognize in each person they meet a child of God who needs and deserves love and care. As the *Catechism* says:

> The entire Christian life bears the mark of the spousal love of Christ and the Church. Already Baptism, the entry into the People of God, is a nuptial mystery; it is so to speak the nuptial bath, which precedes the wedding feast, the Eucharist.[4]

In Saint Paul's letter to Ephesians, we read:

> Husbands, love your wives, even as Christ loved the church and handed himself over for her to sanctify her, cleansing her by the bath of water with the word, that he might present to himself the church in splendor, without spot or wrinkle or any such thing, that she might be holy and without blemish. (5:25–27)

Baptism is the sacrament that applies the mystery of the covenant, the mystery of the nuptial unity between God and humanity, between Christ and the church, to the person. In the baptismal font, the union of Christ and the believer is accomplished in a mystic union that will be perfected in the Eucharist. Baptism is the wedding gift bestowed by Christ to every believer.

In *Familiaris Consortio* we read: "The communion between God and His people finds its definitive fulfillment in Jesus Christ, the Bridegroom who loves and gives Himself as the Savior of humanity, uniting it to Himself as His body."[5]

Here, baptism is represented as the act of Christ who unites himself, in his mystical body, with every baptized person. Through the water and the Holy Spirit, the believer receives the gift of a new, loving relationship with Christ, of which human marriage is only a symbol. Baptism shows us how every child of God belongs to God and is part of the body of Christ rather than living apart and distant from him.

The spouses extend and continue what happens in baptism. After a child or adult is united to Jesus and in a spousal relationship becomes part of his body, she is welcomed by the parents-spouses and continues to live inside the environment created by the parental relationship. This welcoming into the Christian family is what makes real the love of Jesus for his church.

The newly baptized person is like the new life of a small plant, placed into a spousal greenhouse where the Trinitarian warmth of creation, together with the warmth of Christ's union with the church, provides love and nurture. United with the body of Jesus, the newly baptized person is placed inside the sacrament of marriage, which actualizes the love of Jesus for the church.

The sacrament of marriage provides all that is needed to help the child of God mature. Even at a purely human level, it is not a simple thing to bring a person to maturity. A personal presence is necessary, beginning with a mother who nurses a child at her breast, to help the child mature physically and emotionally. Likewise, the child of God who is born in baptism needs something else: he needs to be placed in the Trinitarian greenhouse, in the warmth of the love of Christ and his church that will enable him to grow and develop.

The baptized person is welcomed into the small church where he can breathe the air of the Holy Spirit. The Spirit, with the spouses, comprises the domestic trinity and joins the entire family to Jesus and his universal church. But this Trinitarian and christological climate, which helps the baptized person grow in his uniqueness, is oriented not only to the child of the spouses, but to *every* child of God, to every baptized person who comes into the life of the spouses, regardless of age. This is done through the strength of the sacrament of marriage and does not rely upon the spouses themselves.

In this mysterious power, spouses discover their potential to help the children of God to grow and mature. Spouses are called not only to care for the physical needs, but to make known the love of God to his children.

Imagine a mother who, seeing a small child, remembers with joy her experience of bringing a child into the world and, in love, raising it to maturity. In the same way a married couple—who represents the love of Christ for the church—instinctively understands how each person they encounter is filled with human and divine life, a child of their heavenly Father, destined for union with the Father through the Son.

Every Christian married couple, in the grace of the sacrament of marriage, has received the task of growing and distributing spiritual nourishment for each baptized person they encounter. As an incarnation of the love of Christ for the church—which means love for any baptized person—they manifest the love of Christ in their home and to their neighbors, a love and warmth which every baptized man and woman needs to know and feel.

Through the married couple, God says to each of us, "You are my child." He says this as if each of us were his only child, because each of us is unique to him. The couple has in itself not only mother's milk but also the milk of Christ; it can distribute not only material bread but also spiritual bread. Every couple is not only mother and father to their own children, but also parent to all baptized people. The spouses, in fact, contain the love of Christ for the church and the love of Christ for every baptized person. This helps us to understand the connection between the baptismal liturgy of the church and the married couple: as spouses, they are mother/father of every child passing their home and of every person they meet in the workplace. They are mother/father because inside they have the desire of Christ to help the children of God to grow. Spouses must come to understand themselves as distributors of the parental warmth and care of God for each of his children.

The liturgy of baptism celebrated by the church continues when married couples and parents praise the Father as they encounter each unique person. Every greeting, every kindness, every gesture of attention and care, is no longer just good manners or friendliness. It is given because we desire to honor the Father. The Father has poured out his tenderness on this child and with him we want to share in the joy of welcoming the child to salvation. Sanctification flows from these gifts of love and welcoming that come from God and transform the most ordinary encounters into liturgical acts. When we greet, welcome, offer coffee, or share a meal, we are participating in a liturgy that honors baptism and expresses the warmth and love of Christ for every child of God.

EDUCATION CONTINUES
BAPTISMAL LITURGY

Baptism means, for a child, new life, a new identity that, through the eyes of faith, is visible to those who have known the love of the Father. It is a new life that needs help—continuous presence and focused attention—to grow. All the gestures and words that will cause the new life to grow are a continuation of the baptismal liturgy. Small acts, like feeding, bathing, or changing a diaper, are part of drawing the child into the Trinitarian warmth of the family, an echo of baptism realized through the domestic liturgy. At the center is Jesus Christ—the same Jesus who, through the marriage bond, has united the two parents to himself, and through baptism has united that child to himself. In the family, Jesus is building an extraordinary unity between them and with them.

Christocentric Education[6]

It is Jesus who baptizes; through Christ every baptized person is joined as a living member of his body. It is also Jesus Christ who is present with the spouses, who has united them in marriage, ensuring his presence between them. Jesus must also be the main actor in education. In this way, united to Jesus in baptism, in a home where the spouses are joined to Jesus through the sacrament of marriage, the baptized person continues to encounter the same Jesus to which she was joined in baptism.

Educating to the Presence of Jesus

We need to think about all the signs that demonstrate and manifest the presence of Jesus. Religious symbols—a statue of the Virgin Mary, a crucifix, the image of a saint—can be supports to faith, but they are fixed and motionless. Jesus is alive in our homes. He is not an image or a statue. He is the resurrected Jesus, more alive than we are. The living Jesus is the heart of the family's truth, the heart of the domestic church, the heart of the church itself, and the absolute core of our faith.

Domestic liturgy is any gesture and word that consciously expresses the presence of Jesus. He is in the center of the spouses' lives, both for them and their children, who are aware that they are all one with Jesus. Simple everyday activities such as keeping an empty chair around the table, a lighted candle, or a fresh flower to indicate the presence of Jesus can act as a liturgical reminder. Remembering to consciously greet each other in the morning, thanking and praising the Lord Jesus because he is alive and present—these all are gestures of domestic liturgy that help to celebrate the presence of Christ in the ordinariness of the Bethlehem and Nazareth of Jesus' public life.

Taken together, these small, ordinary gestures are really living out the kingdom of heaven. How many liturgical gestures are made in church to express the presence of Jesus: "The Lord be with you," at the beginning of a Mass, the incensing of the altar to say that Jesus is alive and present, the incensing of the crucified Christ, the priest who kisses the altar at the beginning and end of the Mass? All of these gestures, when consciously undertaken, make the presence of Christ real to the priest and to the community. It is the same for the domestic liturgy: every small action can point to the presence of Jesus.

Educating to the Easter of Jesus

Educating oneself in the Easter of Jesus means taking part in his path of death and resurrection. Through baptism the child is joined to and takes part in the death and resurrection of Jesus. Saint John Paul II teaches, "Spouses are therefore the permanent reminder to the Church of what happened on the Cross; they are for one another and for the children witnesses to the salvation in which the sacrament makes them sharers."[7]

The baptismal rite illustrates how the child is joined through baptism in the death and resurrection of Jesus. In the early centuries, the person who was to be baptized was immersed in water to symbolize his descent into Christ's death.

At the same time, the spouses, by the grace of the sacrament of marriage, make real and visible the total self-giving of Jesus and the rising from death to new life. The death and rising of baptism and the self-donation of the spouses represents a sort of paschal harmony between the parents/spouses and the children. These two expressions of Jesus' sacrifice should be understood as a means of unity within the family and as a continuation of the sacrament of baptism. Parents and children must put into action those gestures that express the shared meanings of death and rising to new life represented in the sacraments of baptism and marriage. In the life of the spouses, as well as in the education of children in the Easter of Jesus, there is a continuous, loving giving, going toward total self-donation, loving even when love is not reciprocated, up to loving one's enemies: "For if you love those who love you, what recompense will you have? Do not the tax collectors do the same?" (Matt. 5:46). The domestic liturgy of giving, of losing, of giving up the body and pouring out the blood for love—like, in its own way, the Eucharist—can be celebrated in the home through real liturgies of renouncement for love, and liturgies of resurrection, for expressing love, for embracing the uniqueness of each life.

Every gesture and act of love, given because Jesus is alive, for sacrificing, for losing, for love, all become gestures of domestic liturgy in continuity with the baptismal liturgy. Through these actions, new identity is expressed and a pathway to life that begins with baptism opens.

Educating to Express and Participate in the Priesthood of Jesus

The "priesthood of all believers" is well-illustrated in *Lumen gentium*:

> Christ the Lord, High Priest taken from among men (cf. Hebrews 5:1–5), made the new people "a kingdom and priests to God the Father" (Revelation 1:6; cf. 5:9–10). The baptized, by regeneration and the anointing of the Holy Spirit, are consecrated as a spiritual house and a holy priesthood, in order that through all those works which are those of the Christian man they may offer spiritual sacrifices and proclaim the power of Him who has called them out of darkness into His marvelous light (cf. Peter 2:10). Therefore all the disciples of Christ, persevering in prayer and praising God (cf. Acts 2:42–47), should present themselves as a living sacrifice, holy and pleasing to God (cf. Romans 12:1).[8]

In simple words, this means that the baptized participate in the whole life of Jesus. Jesus is the one who offers himself to the Father and lives the priesthood. Unlike the Jews of the Old Testament, people no longer offer sacrifices in the temple. All believers have become a priestly community that can "offer spiritual sacrifices pleasing to God." The first sacrifice that Jesus offers is himself, and we are called to make the same sacrifice. Jesus' sacrifice implies that spiritual sacrifice is at the center of family life, and that the liturgy of self-donation, in and with Jesus, is for the praise and glory of the Father and the sanctification of humanity. In this way, we can educate ourselves and others to transform our lives into a prayer of praise to the Father, and to welcome the salvation coming from him.

Belonging to a People

The liturgy can also be expressed by belonging to a we that praises the Lord, to a family that becomes a small priestly assembly. It is the domestic *we*—the *we* of parents, children, and friends who offer praise to the Lord—who listen to his Word as we prepare for the eucharistic *we* of the Sunday assembly. Christians must become builders of an open belonging to which the child will gradually be introduced.

Educating to the Word and Gestures of Jesus

Jesus is present in the life of the couple and family, and he is not silent. He provides his Word, and the children of God are called to listen to and recognize it, just like they recognize the voices of their father and mother. In the rite of the baptism, this is represented by the gestures of touching the ears and the lips, and the words: *Ephphatha*, "that you may praise the Lord and listen to His Word." This is just the opening to the Word. The education to the Word, through its reading and proclamation, is a liturgy that helps us to recognize the voice of Jesus. It also educates children to the fact that Jesus is continuously present through his Word. In this way, children learn that what Jesus says is the most important word, the definitive word, the word that never lies, the word that makes known the true purpose of every baptized person. In marriage, the Word assumes a further meaning: it is the Word of Jesus, the Bridegroom, who wants to speak to the lover, the couple, the one-flesh bride.

EUCHARIST: THE *TELOS* OF EVERY EDUCATIONAL DIMENSION

The Eucharist is the apex of the presence of Jesus, the place where the baptized person touches the highest point of Jesus' earthly vocation. The eucharistic celebration is marriage in fullness. It is also the highest point of being a body, church, or assembly, as well as the highest point of being a child. Looking at the Eucharist, we discover the significance of baptism in creating an expansive and inclusive family. We are not baptized to be children of our father and our mother; we are baptized to be one body in Jesus. In Jesus we form the family of the children of God.

The Sunday liturgy helps the baptized person see this big family. Think for a moment about how many gestures parents have to make to educate children in the recognition of the big family, and at the same time how far they are from their ideals. Many attending the Sunday Mass do so only to accomplish a rite. However, they must see it instead as a family reunion, a feast for the extended family: grandparents, uncles, nephews, relatives, friends. This family enjoys the enlarged feast as part of an even larger family that transcends time: the communion of saints.

GESTURES AND WORDS IN DOMESTIC LITURGY: ACTUALIZING BAPTISM

We now provide some practical suggestions for actualizing the sacrament of baptism.

First is the importance of listening to the Word, which helps us recognize the presence of Jesus. The Word is a liturgical pathway that leads to growth in Jesus. Along with the weekday relationship with the Word, its proclamation is especially important during moments in family and personal life.

Second, we must pay close attention to praying in the name of the Lord in whom we are one body. This prayer is a celebration of the couple's unity in the presence of parents, children, and guests. Through it we are recognized as a community of God's children. Such prayer revives the bond between the family and Jesus and the family and the Father.

Prayer must be nurtured, taught in all its expressions, through prayers of adoration, praise and thanksgiving, and intercession. It must be distributed across the domestic liturgy: mealtime, morning, and before bed. Prayer in the family is an echo of and preparation for the Sunday eucharistic liturgy.

The third practical way of actualizing baptism is in celebrating the love of the entire family—parents and children—as well as the wider family of friends and colleagues, which make up the "big family." Welcome must be practiced as a way to create a true family. A true family is more than just parents and children living separately. A true family is one that opens its doors; shares its love with the world; and, in so doing, creates a family of God that transcends time. The creation of this larger family shows both the roots and the destiny of the individual and the family itself.

A fourth way of celebrating baptism is to remember it as the anniversary of our birth into eternal life. Baptismal anniversaries are rarely noticed, much less celebrated. But doing so helps children and adults grow in the awareness of their dignity as children of God. (By contrast, we do celebrate birthdays without ever reflecting that each passing birthday leads us toward death.) Baptism marks the day of our entrance into eternal life, the day on which we are able to say, "I will forever be a child of God."

Our places of work are also opportunities to build relationships, share the gospel of Christ, and expand the fraternity of the children of God.

In addition to these suggestions for activities related to everyday life, there are also very simple personal gestures for proclaiming the liturgy within the family. It is common to raise one's hands during the Our Father. But this action can be undertaken at any time during the day. Extending the arms toward the sky indicates the desire for relationship with the Father in the same way a child seeks the comfort and embrace of a mother or father on earth. Raising hands toward the sky before your own child can be a way of saying to God, "Lord, I want to be the means of your blessing on this child."

Another gesture is to be conscious of closing the door of the home, while acknowledging the presence of the Lord inside the home and the way in which he links parents and children into one body. Of course, it is important to pray with children, invoking God's blessing on them; in the morning or in the evening when they go to bed, and making the sign of the cross on their forehead. Spouses should also invoke blessing on one another to reaffirm the unique priestly bond they enjoy as the result of the continuing sacrament of their marriage.

Continuation of the baptismal liturgy in the home will grow to the degree that we seek to recover the dignity, strength, and power of baptism as part of a baptismal domestic liturgy. These practices are only the beginning of expressions that spouses, because of their faith, will be able to invent on their own. In the simplicity of the home—as in Nazareth—spouses, children, and the large family of friends and neighbors will, through these gestures, discover and grow in the gift of being children of God.

Chapter 3

CONFIRMATION
and
THE LITURGY OF THE FAMILY

CONFIRMATION: THE SACRAMENT NEEDED TO CELEBRATE MARRIAGE

In this chapter we will examine the meaning of confirmation in the life of a married couple and the family. Our purpose is to highlight the continuity between the sacrament of confirmation and the day-to-day life of the family.

In the *Catechism* we read: "Confirmation brings an increase and deepening of baptismal grace." The word itself, *confirmation*, signifies an act that fulfills and strengthens what happened in baptism. According to the *Catechism*, confirmation roots us more deeply in the divine filiation, which makes us cry, "Abba! Father!"; it unites us more firmly to Christ; it increases the gifts of the Holy Spirit in us.[1]

The *Code of Canon Law* asks that the spouses, before the celebration of marriage, receive the sacrament of confirmation.[2] This could appear to be only a matter of procedural coherence, but in fact it is very meaningful. Through confirmation the baptized are more fully joined to the paschal mystery found in the death and resurrection of Jesus. In confirmation, the baptized take part more intimately in the self-giving of Jesus—including his death and resurrection.

Confirmation enables each of us to give our life for him, as Jesus did for us. Engaged couples need this sacrament for their marriage in order to live in and with Jesus, and to be a total gift for the other through the sacrament of marriage.

Confirmation enables the husband and wife to totally give themselves to each other spiritually. It supports them by forming them more fully in the image of Jesus, who totally donates himself in the Eucharist and on the cross. If, in marriage, a couple wants to make themselves a total gift to each other, then it is in confirmation that they receive the qualification that spiritually prepares them to do so. Only through the Spirit can spouses donate themselves to each other as Jesus donated himself. With the sacrament of marriage, the spouses celebrate the Easter of self-donation that continues for their entire life together.

THE SPOUSES AND THEIR CONFIRMATION

The sign of confirmation, according to the *Catechism*:

> . . . imprints on the soul an indelible spiritual mark, the "character," which is the sign that Jesus Christ has marked a Christian with the seal of his Spirit by clothing him with power from on high so that he may be his witness.[3]

The spiritual mark of confirmation says: "This belongs to God." In the sacrament of marriage, the Holy Spirit, poured out on the spouses, consecrates the new way through which they are called to live their Christian testimony. The couple's witness is connected to the sacrament of marriage, but they are witnesses *in the strength of confirmation.* For in the sacrament of marriage they are called to express the chrismal power of Jesus *together,* as a couple.

Each of us is called to live out our confirmation, which means being witnesses of Jesus up to shedding our blood. A priest is called to live confirmation, but in the *priestly* way. Similarly, the spouses are called to live as baptized and confirmed, but in the *conjugal* way.

In this light, we can look at the effects of confirmation. The *Catechism* says: "The effect of the sacrament of Confirmation is the special outpouring of the Holy Spirit as once granted to the apostles on the day of Pentecost."[4]

Moreover, "confirmation gives us a special strength of the Holy Spirit to spread and defend the faith by word and action as true witnesses of Christ, to confess the name of Christ boldly, and never to be ashamed of the Cross."[5]

The *Catechism* points out how little we understand confirmation and how little we use the power of the Spirit that is in us. To share our faith, we usually rely only on our own energy and organizational and communication skills rather than on the Holy Spirit. All confirmed persons have a prophetic mission to spread the gospel![6] It is the prophetic mission of each baptized and confirmed person to spread the gospel.

The spouses, in the strength of the sacrament of marriage, are called to make visible their particular expression of the good news. Through the gift of the Holy Spirit in marriage, the liturgy celebrated in the rite of confirmation continues in the domestic life. It is a liturgy of continuity, echo, and manifestation. The sacrament of marriage asks the spouses to witness in this specific way. What makes the testimony of spouses different than that of a single baptized person?

HOW SPOUSES INCARNATE
THE GIFT OF THE SPIRIT

Indissoluble Love

First is the absolute unity of the one-flesh and one-Spirit union. By virtue of their lives together, spouses witness to a love that never surrenders. The Lord loves this indissoluble love and wants Christian spouses to shout it as a word of hope to a dying world!

Spouses are called to express total, self-sacrificing love at all times. Their unique contribution is to show a love that never surrenders and that is able to lay down its own life on behalf of another. Even when couples are not physically near, the bond they experience calls them into relationship with one another in their thoughts and prayers. A husband and wife, though apart, think to themselves, "Where is he?" "What is she going to do?" "He has not called me yet." "Why does not she call me?" "He should arrive soon."

The married couple's love is always connected in a reciprocity that is created by their mutual relationship. The conjugal relationship is the substance of the love that can never be missed.

Fertile Love

Another specific testimony of spousal love is fertility. Spouses are called to manifest the loving face of God as father and mother. The physical fertility of marriage is a sign of spiritual fertility necessary to make a family of the children of God. We are all called to this type of fertility, but a powerful source of this exists in a married couple. It is not primarily found in priests or nuns; in them we see only a reflection of fertility. A single priest can tell the parable of the prodigal son, welcoming sinners home to the church. Those in religious life are able to be spiritual fathers and mothers, but who in a community can say better than anyone else that God *is* father and mother? Husbands and wives should manifest to everyone they meet that they are the face of the heavenly Father. The priest should say: "Look at the fathers and the mothers of this community and you will see the face of God!"

Trinitarian-like Love

The married couple lives an explicitly Trinitarian kind of love. This is the love into which everyone is joined in baptism, and the love that confirmation restates. Confirmation reminds us, and reaffirms in us, that everyone is created in the image and likeness of God.

In the spouses, who are simultaneously two persons and yet one flesh, the Lord has given us a model of Trinitarian communion. Of course, this reference is an analogy, which preserves the infinite distance between the creature and the Creator. In the human family, we have God's model for understanding how to make community. There is not a community of nuns or priests or single laypeople so beautiful that it is able to say: "Ours is the model of family that God wants!" The family—at its most ordinary and most natural, which tries to live well—is the model of communion, community, and reciprocal love.

In his *Letter to Families*, Saint John Paul II affirms: "The divine 'We' is the eternal pattern of the human 'we.'"[7] And in the encyclical *Deus Caritas Est*, Benedict XVI writes, "The love of a man and a woman constitutes the archetype of love par excellence."[8]

If I, as a priest (or indeed, any consecrated person), want to understand how to love the community, the church, humanity, *I must look at the love between man and woman*. The family is the model for the church. Jesus himself refers to this model when he asks, "Who are my mother and [my] brothers?" (Mark 3:33). The church and parish are often called a "family of families," because the family is both model and reference point for making a community.

The family continues its prophecy, its chrismal witness, in a permanent state of prophetic mission. This is particularly important in contemporary culture because of the great distress that affects the family. It is more and more difficult to sustain families, and they are less and less united and more and more broken. This means that the prophetic identity of the Christian family is becoming easier to see, and it is of increasing importance. It announces to the world that love is possible, communion is possible, and that total self-donation is possible in the name of love.

If Christian families were a "light of prophecy" to the world, if they were aware of how they shine the light of God's love, they would greatly build church and society! But today this isn't happening. The real danger today for Christian families is that they live this gift in *privacy*, like a "hidden talent" (see Matthew 25:14–20). These families are good only for themselves and live without a testimony to the world, because for them the most important thing is "feeling well among us." This thwarts the family's mission to share Jesus, which was given in baptism and deepened in confirmation.

The Christ-Church Model of Love

Finally, in the grace of the sacrament of marriage, the Spirit leads spouses to live—and to manifest to the church and the world—the higher unity between Christ and the church. Through their chrismal mandate, spouses bear witness to the covenant of love established in the blood of Christ. This covenant is celebrated, and we can admire and contemplate it, in every Mass.

All these dimensions of spousal testimony and prophecy have never received a ritual formalization. They call us to an ordinariness that is extraordinary: the unity and Trinity of God, and the redemption carried out in the incarnation, passion, death, and resurrection of Jesus. When seen in the light of Nazareth, the Christian family is understood as a hidden word and rite, one that contains an immense sanctifying power. Christ's first thirty years in Nazareth are not celebrated in any rite of the church, but they are the highest rite lived by the incarnated Word of God. They give depth to all the ordinary life of spouses and families. Even without a formal rite, this ordinariness is rich with life.

Aware of the Holy Spirit's movement, spouses prepare their child for confirmation and seek ways to initiate him to this gift. As parents perceive and live the presence of the Holy Spirit in their married life, they will know how to educate the child to live and to share his testimony in the strength of confirmation. As much as they understand the preciousness of the gift of the Spirit in married life, they will know how to communicate to the child the importance of preparing for the chrismal rite and of nurturing all that follows from it.

CONFIRMATION: ALL PEOPLE ARE A GIFT FOR THE CHURCH AND THE WORLD

Every single person inside a family is a gift for the whole church and the world. Confirmation "roots us more deeply in the divine filiation [childhood, sonhood, daughterhood], it unites us more firmly to Christ, it increases the gifts of the Holy Spirit in us, it renders our bond with the church more perfect."[9] This passage helps us understand how confirmation brings a change of life and a full maturity to our being in Christ. Confirmation is the sign that Jesus Christ has marked a Christian with the seal of his Spirit by clothing him with power from on high so that the Christian may be Christ's witness.[10]

Confirmation is fullness of life given to every believer according to his gifts. Confirmation does not make all Christians identical to the Holy Spirit. Rather, through confirmation, the Holy Spirit helps us understand that inside the visible physical and psychological diversity of every person, is also spiritual diversity and originality. Each has his or her own gift in the church for the world. The gift of the Holy Spirit empowers Christians to the fullest, to make visible that particular aspect of Jesus and his action in the church that dwell in the spiritual DNA of every baptized and confirmed person.

God creates life so that, through the unique beauty of a child, he can announce a singular word of blessing to the world. The same is true between husband and wife; they can ask the questions, "Why did God create my spouse to be part of this world? What particular beauty does God wish to speak through this woman or man?" If it is difficult to see this, after many years of ordinary life, it is even more difficult to see the specific gift received by a child during his growth.

CELEBRATION OF CONFIRMATION IN ORDINARINESS

There is a liturgy of birth, of baptism, of confirmation, and of sharing of gifts. These are celebrated in ordinariness that makes these gifts grow in their beauty and uniqueness. The following are very simple examples of how a domestic liturgy could be celebrated to help a confirmed child grow in his or her own uniqueness.

In the domestic liturgy, a little child learns to say "daddy" or "father." And, by repetition, this idea is imprinted on the heart. A mother and father experience great satisfaction as they help the child to grow and recognize God as Father. Through this liturgy, which connects the earthly parents to the Father in heaven, the child learns that he will never be alone, even when the parents die, because he will understand that he is loved and cared for by his heavenly Father.

In this liturgy of ordinariness, parents also help the child to grow spiritually and express his or her beauty. Parents must be interested not only in the child's intellectual capabilities and physical skills but, along with them, have a faithful desire to bring out from the children their spiritual characteristics.

As they grow, many children display a beautiful spiritual imprint; in others, though, this imprint is completely absent. They lack a face. Why? Who was charged to cultivate the face of spiritual beauty in this child? Parents have a wonderful opportunity, through the warmth of spiritual incubation in the Trinitarian greenhouse, to bring out from children their spiritual characteristics in ordinary life, with patience, over a long period of time. These are precious years as parents strive to understand the kind of fruit that will be born from that small tree when it is grown. Christian parents must not only educate children to have a role in society, to hold a job, but they must also educate them to be a gift for the church and the world as faithful witnesses of Jesus.

How frequently we ask a child: "What would you like to do when you grow up?" And how many times do we as parents say, "I would like my child to have this job . . . or become this type of person." How rarely do we say, "I would like my child to be a witness of Jesus, my daughter to be a blessing to the church"?

This type of education cannot be given during a short period of vocational training. It is a liturgical and educational pathway that passes through baptism, confirmation, and Eucharist. Walking this pathway within a family, with a father and mother, helps the child to grow into his spiritual beauty and identity: being like Jesus, full of life and humanity.

THE BODY: RECURRING THEME OF DOMESTIC CELEBRATIONS

We celebrate our domestic liturgy in our physical bodies, from baptism to confirmation. We know that the body of the child is from birth the starting point of communication, for the giving and receiving of joy between the child and others. We remember the joy of a little child when he shows his family his ability to move, shares what he sees, and develops language, all of which he uses to communicate with the world around him. We need to contemplate the beauty of this child who welcomes challenges as he tries to communicate: *if I smile at him, he smiles at me. If I move, then he moves. If I run away, then he chases me.* This is how the body is used for communication, and what a satisfaction for the parents to witness this fullness of communication between them and their child's body!

As the body matures and becomes aware of itself, it is helped in this task by others. It is a body that is made not only for receiving, but also for donating, for giving. The child understands that his actions can be a gift for the other, or that he can refuse to give of himself. In this way, he is gradually initiated to the reality that the overall communicative system of a person, of a body, is made to receive and to give love.

The patient cultivation, education, and celebration of this knowledge creates in a person the understanding that God is love and that we are made in his image and likeness. Our psycho-physical structure is made for loving. Our likeness to God is not found in similar eye color, but in being able to love like him! Therefore, after a child has developed communication skills, he is led to discover that this communication is for the communica-tion of love. Thus, the gesture becomes a caress and a welcome to return the caress. The child learns to receive and give.

The communicative potential of the body is perfected further during childhood and teen years, when the individual learns he is able not only to give and to receive, but that he has a body that is made to love. This capacity for love is not just in his sexuality; it is his body that has unlimited possibilities to give love to and receive love from everyone. At this stage, some imperfections in earlier stages of development may emerge as distortions in how the individual loves. For example, the child or youth starts to select friends and circumstances only because they are to his liking. In this behavior, the young person seeks only for a positive response or gratification of the desire for love. This type of love is transactional: "I give to you and you give to me." Cultivating the habit of transactional love is a most serious risk, especially if the youth has not received a proper pre-education. Essentially, this leads to identifying love with being loved and leads people to search for love. In this context, loving gestures are only for provoking and for receiving love, rather than for communicating love within that seeks to express itself. It is love as attention-seeking.

This kind of love is completely turned in on itself. It is the end of love, because love is itself a gift, a kind of losing to give. From this perspective, the current educational atmosphere is openly anti-chrismal, because it mostly educates to receive love. Consider how little children are over-coddled, showered with gifts—presents and toys enough to fill rooms—and yet still seek more. Children become aggressive in asserting themselves, demanding space and attention at the expense of others, up to tormenting fathers and mothers for having brought them into the world. Receiving becomes synonymous with existence. It is not, "I am because I love," but rather, "I am because I receive." It is clear from attitudes like this, expressed in the body, that youth can eventually seek *only* to receive.

This attitude heightens the difficulty of the last stage, when the young adult reaches maturity in love: "I have a body made for loving, and I want to give it." In the final analysis, the apex of love is being completely a gift, a love that no longer needs to receive. Ask a father or mother what the apex of love is, or an elderly person in a nursing home. They will tell you that the apex of love is to give.

Take, for example, a mother and her child: What is the apex of love for a mother? Love is to give rather than receive. In fact, even if the child calls the parents once a month, a mother and a father are always ready to rush to give everything. The same is true for husband and wife when they live their most intense affective moments: the best of them comes out when they are completely giving themselves, losing themselves, even dying to themselves.

A young man who reaches the apex of love will say, "I have a body made for love, and I want to give it." If he does not reach this state of self-giving, he will ask, "How much are you able to give me?" How can one be like Jesus, who completely donated himself, without arriving at this place? It is the full donation of the self that fulfills a person in being created in the image and likeness of God, of being marked by the Holy Spirit in confirmation. This total self-giving as a confirmed Christian conforms the Christian completely to Jesus.

This is the vocational moment. After these different stages (body for communicating, body for loving, body for donating), I am called by Jesus to join myself to his self-donation. I can realize my union with God by giving myself to my spouse and, through and with Jesus, being a gift for the church and the world. It may appear that the vocation of marriage is only for donating one's body for love to a man or a woman, but this is just another step in the journey of giving oneself completely to God. Every baptized and confirmed person is called to this task, whether single or married. The unmarried can give themselves singularly to Jesus and the church. In marriage, the husband and wife give themselves to one another and, together, to the church and the world.

This is the vocational domestic liturgy, which does not consist of celebrating weddings in homes but rather in helping children to understand, day-by-day, their vocation.

We could say, therefore, that the domestic liturgy is the "liturgy of the fragment" or the "liturgy of the flowing river." It is not a Niagara Falls. It is not the celebration of an extraordinary rite, in the presence of all the people of God, but a river slowly flowing among everyday life and activities.

While every liturgical act is the celebration of the mystery of Jesus' salvation, the domestic liturgy is a flowing river of sanctification. It is the long love story of God for his people; it is no longer connected to only one act, but to an endless set of gestures and words, the long history of salvation that leads to the fullness of the gift received by everyone.

CONFIRMATION: CELEBRATING THE UNITY OF THE HOLY SPIRIT AND THE UNIQUENESS OF PEOPLE

The Holy Spirit, given to parents and children through the sacrament of confirmation, makes it possible for the family to celebrate and manifest an extraordinary, divine unity. Between parents and children, who breathe the same Holy Spirit and express the same love, a unity is realized that goes beyond blood relationships and raises unity to extraordinary heights. In fact, unity in the Holy Spirit is higher than unity between father and son, and bride; it is unity in God that transcends the family alone. We need, therefore, to identify some celebrative moments of this unity that transcend all disagreements, differences, and distances—male-female, young-old, and all generational gaps. It is important to help all the family's members experience and enjoy this unity, and extend it to other people who encounter the family.

This powerful unity in the Spirit can be celebrated, lived, and shared in prayer, but also in contemplating and praising a beautiful thing, a family event, a sunset, a natural vista. In these moments, a family experiences a unity that is given not only by the thing done or observed or by the ties of blood, but even more by the Holy Spirit's presence. As they sit around the table after a meal, sharing affection and conversation, they celebrate the union between the couple and between parents and children. These ordinary times are a glimpse of heaven.

But alongside this unity, we should take care to pay attention to each family member. It is important to set aside time to recognize and celebrate individual achievements and milestones—a gift received, a grade at school, a sports team victory, or a special insight shared by a family member. In this way, we celebrate and highlight God's grace in the life of each person. In doing so, we educate everyone in the importance of appreciating the beauty of what mother, father, son, daughter, and grandparent are doing. Thus, we highlight the intimate and original beauty of every family member.

This is the life of the family: unity and distinction, unity and originality. The family is called, as a systolic and diastolic system, to have both of these characteristics: beauty in unity and beauty in the distinctiveness and originality of each member.

The Spirit manifests inside the family's life and can help to absorb, appropriate, and understand the received gift. Through the Spirit we are able to understand how our day-to-day life is full of signs that can help transform the family's life into a domestic liturgy.

In the Scriptures three images are frequently used to describe the action of the Holy Spirit: wind, fire, and water. Each of these elements belongs to normal life and does not require a church to be celebrated. In our families we should use them to discover the gift of domestic liturgy. In a strong wind, or a sweet evening breeze, we can feel embraced, wrapped, and caressed, and say, "The Spirit is like this! The Spirit wraps; the Spirit caresses; the Spirit enters the body through breath: the Spirit makes us one."

Or we can imagine a couple, or a family, along a river, or alongside a mountain spring being aware that the Holy Spirit's living water is in the couple or the family.

Finally, we can imagine ourselves around the fireplace. We need to let this fire enter our souls and warm us, to remember how the fire of the Spirit is poured out upon the spouses and upon all confirmed persons. This is the fire the Spirit desires to fan into a blaze just as Jesus said, "I have come to set the earth on fire, and how I wish it were already blazing!" (Luke 12:49).

Chapter 4

THE EUCHARIST
and
THE LITURGY OF
THE FAMILY

In this chapter we deepen our understanding of the connection between the Eucharist and the domestic liturgy.

Jesus Christ presides invisibly over every eucharistic celebration through his body, which is the church. In the eucharistic celebration, every member of the church has a role, starting with the priest who presides over the Eucharist as the visible sign of Jesus. It is Jesus himself who reactualizes his sacrifice and his resurrection to new life. It is Jesus who makes us a part of his eucharistic work—as he did the apostles at the Last Supper—making the mysteries of incarnation, passion, death, and resurrection touch each person who welcomes them. This is an extraordinary mystery of love through which Jesus transcends time and space to make us present with him in the Upper Room, to touch each individual, and to make it possible for us, in body and spirit, to meet the living Lord. In that holy bread, it is he, in person; every mediating element disappears, and that bread is no longer bread, but the resurrected body of Jesus.

WHO IS THE PROTAGONIST IN THE SACRAMENT OF MARRIAGE?

Jesus is also at the center of the sacrament of marriage and is its chief actor. In the sacrament of marriage, Jesus acts through the signs manifested between the two spouses and between parents and children. The self-donation, sacrifice, and resurrection of Christ are made real and present by the spouses in their sacrifice for each other.

The liturgical action that Jesus accomplishes in the Eucharist finds a direct continuation and echo in the life of the couple and family. In the Eucharist, Jesus wants to directly reach every person with his presence, making them his intimate friends. In the sacrament of marriage, Jesus wants to come near, touch, and make his love felt by whomever is still far away from the Upper Room. Through the sacrament of marriage and the permanent state of mutual self-donation between the spouses, Jesus expresses his love for humanity and for the church. Jesus, who lives in absolute love and donation, wants to reach all humanity through the continuous love of the spouses.

What is celebrated in the intimacy of the church's liturgy, Jesus wants to be tasted and enjoyed by those who are not yet part of the assembly. What he says with his body in the church, he wants to echo and extend through the body of the spouses outside the church. The spouses are the visible expression of the invisible presence of Jesus in the Eucharist.

WHAT IS CELEBRATED IN THE EUCHARIST?

The *Catechism* teaches:

> At the Last Supper, on the night he was betrayed, our Savior instituted the Eucharistic sacrifice of his Body and Blood. This he did in order to perpetuate the sacrifice of the cross throughout the

ages until he should come again, and so to entrust to his beloved
Spouse, the Church, a memorial of his death and resurrection.[1]

Eucharist is the memory, actualization, and representation,
objective and real, of the Paschal Christ, given by the Father to
the world for its salvation. Jesus gives himself in a perpetual,
everlasting self-donation to his spouse, the church, for the world.
He has joined his life indissolubly to his church regardless of
how the church responds. Jesus loves the church regardless of its
response or whether it is beautiful or good in a particular
moment. In the same way, spouses are called to love one
another regardless of whether their love is responded to or not.
Eucharist is Jesus giving himself to his bride, the church. With
the church, he continues his passion of love for all humanity
that, through the incarnation, is united to him as his flesh. In
the Eucharist, the identity and mission of Jesus are celebrated
simultaneously. The church celebrates Jesus giving himself
totally—dying, resurrecting, pouring out his Spirit—to continue
his mission to the farthest ends of the earth, telling all people
to "take and eat; this is my body . . . This is my blood of the
covenant, which will be shed for you and for many" (Matt.
26:26; Mark 14:22, 24; Luke 22:19–20; 1 Cor. 11:25).

Being called to receive the Eucharist means taking part in the
redeeming action of Christ. Through the amen, any baptized
person confirms his decision to give himself to Jesus, to join with
him in the Father's love and in his salvific mission to the entire
world. Evangelization and mission are intimately connected
to the Eucharist, because Eucharist is Jesus going to meet his
people. When we fail to engage in this going, we nullify mission
and cancel the purpose of Jesus' donation. Too often, we eat the
Eucharist, give thanks for it, and feel better—but lack the element
of mission and evangelization.

It is like hiding the bride from the bridegroom just after the
wedding. As the bridegroom desires to meet the bride, so Jesus
desires to meet his bride. Why does Jesus give his flesh? To whom

does Jesus give his flesh? To his bride. If we do not let Jesus reach his bride, the world, then we deny him his bride. When we fail to engage in mission, we prevent the embrace of Jesus, full of love for the church and all humanity, which he wants to join to himself.

WHAT IS CELEBRATED IN MARRIAGE?

The celebration of marriage begins with the nuptial rite and continues throughout the whole life of the spouses; thus, it is a permanent sacrament, like the Eucharist. It gives the spouses the gift of a new communion. In *Familiaris Consortio*, Saint John Paul II writes:

> The gift of the Spirit is . . . a stimulating impulse [for spouses' lives] so that every day they may progress towards an ever richer union with each other on all levels—of the body, of the character, of the heart, of the intelligence and will, of the soul—revealing in this way to the Church and to the world the new communion of love, given by the grace of Christ.[2]

Further on we read: "The intimate community of conjugal life and love, founded by the Creator is elevated and assumed into the spousal charity of Christ, sustained and enriched by His redeeming power."[3]

The mutual love of the spouses is drawn up into the spousal love of Christ: spouses are brought into the self-giving of Christ for the church and humanity, into the paschal mystery, and thereby involved in the Eucharist itself.

This is the profound mystery Saint Paul talks about, which creates unlimited spaces for meditation and contemplation, a unique call for spouses to holiness and mission. Again in *Familiaris Consortio*, we read: "Spouses are therefore the permanent reminder to the Church of what happened on the Cross. . . . Of this salvation event marriage, like every sacrament, is a memorial, actuation and prophecy."[4]

Therefore, in a marriage—its life, gestures, and words, in everything that may happen in an ordinary day of conjugal life, from the morning through the evening—the paschal mystery and Jesus' giving of himself are celebrated as part of the permanent sacrament of marriage. Spouses are drawn into the spousal love of Christ: this refers not to some particular gesture accomplished in special circumstances, but to all the ordinary gestures and activities of life—cooking, cleaning, working, embracing, and every other expression of love and service. All the gestures accomplished between bride and bridegroom are drawn up into the spousal charity of Christ, including those that occur in the most difficult moments of suffering.

Jesus goes on in the Eucharist to personally and directly recall his Easter. Married life also recalls and actualizes his Easter, his giving himself, his sacrificing, his struggling, and sometimes his saying: "I cannot go on! Father, why have you forsaken me?" Spouses actualize this paschal giving through their mutual giving to and for the other. There is nothing done in married life that is not done in relationship with and in reference to Christ. And this giving of Jesus inside the life of the couple always has the same purpose: reaching every person the couple encounters with his love.

Earlier, in *Familiaris Consortio*, we read that, "spouses participate in and are called to live the very charity of Christ who gave Himself on the Cross."[5] This kind of love is distributed over the ordinary circumstances of a day—to be patient during a tedious conversation or perform a simple task at the request of a spouse or child. Everything can be lived with the charity of Christ himself.

WHAT IS THE PURPOSE OF
THE EUCHARIST?

In the Eucharist, we celebrate the anticipation; Eucharist makes us live our destiny in advance. By participating in the supper of the eucharistic bread, the Lord Jesus joins us to his resurrected body and brings us out of time to be one with him in the Trinity. He makes us alive in his Spirit to the praise of the Father. Through the Eucharist, here and now, we are involved in the Trinitarian life, through Jesus, that we will live and enjoy in fullness only in the next life. When we become one with Jesus in the Eucharist, we are already in God; we are in eternity, even if still in this life. In the Eucharist, we also meet the brothers and sisters, saints and blessed people who came before us.

Even though our senses do not feel anything extraordinary, in every Eucharist we live in the heavenly dimension. No mystic vision has a value greater than this Communion. Unity with Jesus in the Eucharist surpasses every vision, because in it we are already united with the resurrected body of Christ, even if this unity is not yet fully accomplished.

The *Catechism of the Catholic Church* affirms this:

> The Church knows that the Lord comes even now in his Eucharist and that he is there in our midst. However, his presence is veiled. Therefore we celebrate the Eucharist [as the priest says before the communion] "awaiting the blessed hope and the coming of our Savior, Jesus Christ."[6]

In a veiled way, the Eucharist gives us an experience of the meeting with the Lord in the next life; it projects us into eternity.

EUCHARISTIC CELEBRATION AND ORDINARY DOMESTIC LIFE

Liturgy of the Word

The eucharistic liturgy is called by the Word. Before the banquet of the body and blood of Jesus, there is the banquet of his Word. At the same time, concerning the family, we read from *Familiaris Consortio*: "The family, called together by word and sacrament as the Church of the home, is both teacher and mother, the same as the worldwide Church."[7]

The Word, in the Eucharist, prepares for the banquet. In the same way, marriage is called by the Word, because it is an answer to the Lord's call. In the family, as a mosaic with many small tiles, life itself continuously composes the word that summarizes all Scripture: *love.*

This is affirmed in *Familiaris Consortio:* "The central word of Revelation, 'God loves His people,' is likewise proclaimed through the living and concrete word whereby a man and a woman express their conjugal love."[8]

The liturgies of the Word celebrated in the home are like a responsorial psalm or saying "Alleluia" before the gospel. In the couple and family, there is a continuous liturgy of listening to and proclaiming of the Word, which then realizes itself also in the specific listening to the Word of God and in the reading of the Bible in the family.

Declaration of Faith

In the eucharistic liturgy, the entire people are called to answer the proclamation of the Word through a declaration of faith found in the Creed. In faith alone, we receive the light to distinguish the Word of the Lord from mere words. Only in faith can the gestures made in the eucharistic liturgy, as well as in the domestic one, be understood: faith is the key to interpreting the eucharistic liturgy. Without faith, we cannot understand the Mass. In faith alone we can understand how a man, the priest who celebrates the Mass, can say, "the Word of God," or, "This is my body." Is it even possible to really attend Mass without faith?

Marriage is a faith celebration as well, and very often it requires that one says, "I believe." As the liturgy of the church, through the Creed in the Sunday Eucharist, makes us one, so in the family we often need to say, "I believe in one God, Father, Son, and Holy Spirit." Without this Creed, it is impossible to realize the profound soul of marriage, as well as the expectations and the gift coming from it.

Therefore, every time a husband or wife, facing a difficult moment, says in his or her soul, "I believe! I believe in this sacrament; I believe in the presence of Jesus!" they affirm and celebrate their faith. Only by celebrating faith do spouses discover the eternal source of love of which they are sign and image. Only by celebrating faith do spouses recognize and live the "visible presence" of the invisible love that links God to humanity and Christ to the church. Through this recognition, spouses share with the world a lived and participatory faith.

Eucharistic Offertory

By taking the bread and wine to the altar, the entire assembly declares its participation in all that is lived and offered. By raising these elements up to the sky, the community asks God to act, with his saving and liberating power, upon the assembly and the whole world. Even the tithes and offerings have this meaning as they are placed upon the altar.

For the spouses, *Familiaris Consortio* says: "Their daily lives are transformed into 'spiritual sacrifices acceptable to God through Jesus Christ.'"[9] Every gesture of spouses becomes a spiritual sacrifice.

Eucharistic Consecration

When the Holy Spirit is invoked in the Eucharist, the bread and wine are *transubstantiated.* This theological word means that, by the power of the Holy Spirit, bread and wine are transformed into the body and blood of Jesus. I still see bread and wine, but they are the body and blood of Jesus; a physical transformation occurs, although it is not visible to the eye.

In the life of a married couple, there is another word to express how the permanent sacrament is celebrated in the domestic church: *transfiguration.* In the fourth eucharistic prayer, the Holy Spirit is invoked over the couple: "Transfigure this masterpiece that you have begun in them." This is exactly what continuously happens by the action of the Holy Spirit, if the spouses permit it. It is not a transformation occurring once and for all, but a transformation that involves every moment of every day, through the spouses' free consent.

This movement of the Spirit transfigures human love and gives it a christological nature. It changes ordinary life—hard, ordinary life; sometimes terrible, ordinary life—into a conscious spiritual offering. It transfigures the family dinner table into a proclamation of a bigger supper, the eucharistic one. Ask yourself this: How many times does our domestic table become a desire for Eucharist, desire of another supper, which joins us to more than just a delicious meal? This celebration transfigures the love of the spouses and the family from occasional into definitive and indissoluble. It transfigures suffering, large and small, into the possibility of giving our lives for love. It transfigures every encounter with other people into possibilities to help other children of God to mature. It transfigures our actions from indifferent into meaningful, and from meaningful into actions capable of communicating love.

COMMUNING WITH THE GIVEN BODY: LIVING FULL UNITY WITH THE CRUCIFIED AND RESURRECTED CHRIST

In the Eucharist, we find the apex, the absolute, of communicated love. There is no other experience of love greater than this: Jesus gives us not only something of himself, but *everything* of himself. It is the apex of the realized unity, of which marriage— the union of two bodies—is only a symbol, a sign. Eucharist is the highest liturgy of love, of which spouses, in the limitation of their gestures, are called to echo, make real, and communicate.

Their liturgy of unceasing giving to and receiving of the other will be celebrated with continuity in the everyday things, small and large, stretched out to a unity that is no longer only a harmony of two bodies, but a unity poured out upon them by the Holy Spirit.

How many times spouses can "have communion by themselves." How many times spouses can give themselves to each other!

In *Familiaris Consortio* we read:

> The love between husband and wife and, in a derivatory and broader way, the love between members of the same family—between parents and children, brothers and sisters and relatives and members of the household—is given life and sustenance by an unceasing inner dynamism leading the family to ever deeper and more intense communion, which is the foundation and soul of the community of marriage and the family.[10]

For the spouses, making eucharistic love real in everyday life is not only giving oneself and welcoming the other, but in becoming for the church and humanity bread to be eaten. The family, one can say, must eat and make itself eaten, because the purpose of eating the Eucharist of the family is becoming Eucharist for everyone! My entire life—with family, friends, neighbors, and coworkers—can become a continuous giving of communion.

The family and the spouses are the continuation of Christ's self-giving dressed in human flesh. As Christ is a gift of love, a total gift of himself, so the family becomes a gift of itself. For this reason, the family has the mission, the purpose, "to guard, reveal and communicate love, and this is a living reflection of and a real sharing in God's love for humanity and the love of Christ the Lord for the Church His bride."[11]

HOW IS THE FAMILY CALLED TO GIVE ITSELF?

The Christian family is called upon to place itself, what it is and what it does, as an "intimate community of conjugal life and love,"[12] at the service of the church and of society.

Like the Eucharist, the family gives itself to the church and humanity as communion. The family "communicates its communion" to the world.

What is the greatest gift a family can give to the church and, thus, to society? The most precious thing the spouses have to give is their communion. The family makes communion to the world and takes the Eucharist to the world by giving its communion. But it does this not because it is beautiful or extraordinary, not because it is without suffering. The spouses give a communion of love built on the sacrifice of the cross.

CONCLUSION

The Eucharist is family even when there is no family. People are alone for many reasons: they are without children; one spouse has died; there is a separation or a divorce; even if they live together, there is poor communication between them. Perhaps they are alone because the faith is lived by only one of the two, or in a completely different way.

We draw inspiration for this reflection from Saint John of the Cross. He ended up in ecclesial prison due to conflicts that grew from the reform of the monastery at Carmel. He was imprisoned first in the convent jail, and two months later in another prison purposely prepared for him, and dark and suffocating as a tomb. There he remained for nine months.

His cell was two-and-a-half-by-two meters, with a small window from which he could not even see the light of the sun; he was given only bread and water and left in utter solitude. As punishment, he could not receive the Eucharist. Nevertheless, on the day of Corpus Domini, Saint John composed one of his most beautiful poems, "The Poem of the Fount":[13]

> For I know well the spring that flows and runs,
> although it is night.

> That eternal spring is hidden,
> for I know well where it has its source,
> although it is night.
>
> I know that nothing else is so beautiful,
> and that the heavens and the earth drink there,
> although it is night.

In each verse, he repeats "although it is night," expressing the depths of loss he is experiencing. From the extreme situation to which he is reduced, he contemplates the Eucharist!

In the final verses, he speaks of God who comes down in the Eucharist, and who from there calls all his creatures to him, which are filled with it, though it is still night.

> This eternal spring is hidden
> in this living bread for our life's sake,
> although it is night.
>
> It is here calling out to creatures;
> and they satisfy their thirst, although in darkness,
> because it is night.
>
> This living spring that I long for,
> I see in this bread of life,
> although it is night.

Although it is night, although family seems to disappear, in that bread I find the Bridegroom who has thought about and loved me from the beginning. Although it is night, though solitude grips me even in bed beside my spouse, you are with me in intimacy. You make me think about the spouse beside me, about the time when we will be set free from our sins. Then my beloved spouse, from whom for the moment I feel separated, will appear in the beauty that you have ordained.

Although it is night, without family, abandoned, left alone, you are the anticipation of family restored and fulfilled.

Although it is night, without family, you are anticipating in me the destiny of a loving communion where every unity will be seen in fullness, every division healed, and every solitude become a tri-unity, forever.

Chapter 5

FORGIVENESS

and

THE LITURGY OF THE FAMILY

In this chapter we turn to the sacrament of forgiveness, seeking to celebrate this gift and to understand it in the domestic church of marriage and family.

THE SOURCE OF FORGIVENESS

In the early centuries of Christianity, the sacraments of Christian initiation had a very precise sequence: baptism, confirmation, and Eucharist. He who became a "new man in Christ" through baptism welcomed the gift of the Spirit in confirmation and completed his union with Jesus in the Eucharist (see Colossians 3:10; Ephesians 4:24; Galatians 3:27). The sacrament of reconciliation—*penance*—came later, because it is only after the fullness of eucharistic unity with Jesus that the seriousness of sin becomes clear. The Eucharist helps us understand and feel the weight of sin and, simultaneously, the permanent, living source of forgiveness. The Eucharist is at the heart of the sacrament of forgiveness.

At the Last Supper, Jesus Christ gives himself so completely that he becomes one flesh with his community-bride, the church. He does not deliver himself to his bride only through declarations of love ("I am ready to die for you; I would be ready to do anything"), but through his body. He does not deliver himself into a void or vacuum, but into the hands and the mouths of his little family, which is the beginning of his church.

In his concrete surrendering, Christ already knows Peter's betrayal. "You will deny me three times," he tells Peter (Matt. 26:34). He knows the treachery of Judas and sees how sin distorts all humanity and his church. In these two betrayals, he sees all the betrayals that would ever occur. At the Last Supper, he is refused by two apostles, and at the same time sees all the refusals of human beings throughout time. He knows that he, though without sin, must enter into the drama of sin. In the moments before his final betrayal by Judas, Jesus spontaneously anticipates and delivers himself to everyone.

Judas did not violate the freedom of Jesus, because Jesus gave himself up voluntarily. At the Last Supper, Christ the Bridegroom gave himself to a community who betrays him. He also gave himself *because* the community betrays him. This is an extraordinary mystery: Christ placed himself in the hands of those who reject him. He gave himself to those who deny him and lead him to death.

This dramatic human rejection intensifies Jesus' gift, showing even more clearly its purity, totality, and absolute freedom. It reveals to us the character of Christ's surpassing love, which infinitely exceeds and surpasses the rejection of his community-bride. He anticipates his bride's betrayal by inserting himself inside the betrayal. Thus, through the paradox of his sacrificial love, he makes all of us his community-bride. He forgives and recreates at the same time, and he does so by giving his body and his life.

The other side of betrayal and forgiveness is that of the community-bride. This bride, perhaps without a full knowledge of what she does, welcomes the eucharistic body given up for love. The community acts in an obscure faith, still not aware of what it is experiencing. Nevertheless, it accomplishes an act of faith: it takes, eats, and drinks. The Christ the community members want to betray is within them—and acts in them—despite their betrayal. They bring with them the Christ received in the bread and wine, the victim of their own sin and betrayal. They are living through that life they have put to death. So the body of Christ, through the action of the Spirit, is inside the body of the community-bride, even as it sins.

This is truly entering into the mystery of love and pain. Christ is inside those who betray him. He gives his body to the community-bride who has sinned. Judas and Peter are inside this body, and in them all the sins of all mankind and the church are symbolized. The fact that this nuptial self-giving is celebrated inside the betrayal and denial does not dim or debase it. The betrayal does not detract from love; on the contrary, it emphasizes, amplifies, and authenticates it. The betrayal reveals that the nuptial love of Christ is a love that loves in and beyond death. Death becomes the way of total love, of the most complete devotion. Pure love has overwhelmed sin.

In light of the forgiveness and reconciliation found in the Eucharist, we discover the source of forgiveness in marriage and family. The spouses celebrate the one flesh and become, day-by-day, one in love. The gift of the body implies acceptance of the other regardless of health or age, and it also takes into account the spiritual and moral limitations and defects spouses find in one another.

We could ask: Up to which point do we need to love? Maybe even in betrayal and beyond betrayal? The human response is often immediate, except among those who have understood that love cannot disappear even when the other sins. We know that we are made in the image and likeness of God, and, therefore, have a predisposition to love "in the manner of God." Alongside this little light, there is the mystery of Jesus who loves the church-community. By the grace of the sacrament of marriage, the spouses participate in the same love with which Christ has loved his community-bride.

For Christian couples, the horizon of love is opened and is no longer subject to human calculation. Love has its reference point in the *source* of love and forgiveness, the grace of the sacrament of marriage. Because the Holy Spirit has been poured out on them in the sacrament of marriage, they permanently participate in the love of Jesus for the church and are able to love one another as Christ loves his bride.[1]

As we discovered earlier, the nuptial love of Jesus for his community-bride is the model to which the spouses can compare themselves and which they can hope to become. At the same time, it is also the source of grace and energy that empowers them. The nuptial gift of Jesus bears within it a forgiveness that foresees, comprehends, and overtakes sin. So it is also for spouses.

FOR WHAT WE ASK TO BE FORGIVEN

If the source of forgiveness is the infinite love that has been manifested in Jesus, we must evaluate our sins in light of the surpassing and overwhelming love God gives to each of us. We must comprehend how little we realize what it means to be loved by God and to begin counting the opportunities we have missed to receive and respond to his love. Second, we must also ask whether we are recognizing the presence of Jesus in others and, in honoring that presence, whether we are sharing God's love freely. This is the point on which God will judge us: "I was hungry; I was thirsty," Jesus said (Matt. 25:35). In this way, and only in this way, we can begin to become conscious of sin and be moved to ask for forgiveness.

Too often, we start our journey of forgiveness with other less-important standards. We categorize our sins, naming some more serious than others. Where a revival of love and life is needed, we settle for quieting our consciences through a superficial confession. We measure our repentance by the love we are receiving from God. Instead, we should be asking what God's love—fully recognized, understood, and responded to—calls forth from us and into the world.

This principle is also true in the life of the couple and the family. The true criteria for examining sin are whether and how the husband and wife are expressing their love for each other. Sin is the failure to love.

We also sin when we do not recognize and welcome the signs of spousal love. Not seeing and receiving the love of our spouse is itself sin, but it has the further, deeper effect of depriving the one-flesh union of the spouses (that new person created by and through marriage) of the love that can nourish and strengthen it. The more we know that love is beyond any measure of value we possess and is part of the infinite and eternal God from which it comes, the more we understand how great our sin is when we fail to see and respond to love.

Again, sin is not a matter of things done or not done, but of not seeing and responding to love. Love is the great commandment. The failure of one spouse to love does not justify the failure of the other spouse to love. Often, even without meaning to, we reduce love to a system of barter or exchange, of loving only in return for love. This understanding of love corrodes, and eventually destroys, the very love it seeks.

Conscious of the infinite and imperative nature of love, the couple can begin to understand whether they are truly seeing, receiving, and giving the love of Jesus in their married life. This love finds its source not in the couple themselves, but first and foremost in the love of Jesus and the way the couple responds to it. The couple's love—rooted in, and sustained and strengthened by the love of Jesus in their life—then spills into their entire network of relationships and their broader community. This kind of love cannot, by its nature, do otherwise. Conversely, not understanding and responding to this love impairs and limits the couple both within and beyond the family.

ACCEPTING FORGIVENESS IS ASKING FOR FORGIVENESS

In the previous section, we explored Jesus as the source of forgiveness and how he gave himself freely at the very moment of betrayal.

Jesus, Son of God, seeks and accomplishes, with our free response, a full and total unity between him and us. In the Eucharist, we realize spiritual marriage between Creator and creature. It is higher than any other form of marriage, a union between the infinity of God and the human fragment. In the light of this wedding offered by Jesus, of this unity enacted by Jesus, and the poverty of our individual and communal responses, the depth of our personal and community betrayal emerges.

Before the Bridegroom Jesus, we are each like the publican in the temple, who beats his chest as he comes to realize the depth of his sin. We can only stand before him like Zacchaeus, who descends from the tree of his justification, and realizes his need to respond to Jesus' love. Or, like Peter on the shore of the lake, who in the knowledge of his betrayal does not dare to explain or justify himself. Before the proposal of Jesus, "Peter, do you love me? Do you love me more than these? Do you love me?" he dares not argue (John 21:15). Naked before the risen Son of God, he says: "Lord, you know" (John 21:17).

So Jesus, the lover who falls in love with us before we are able to fall in love with him, has instituted the sacrament of the Eucharist to join each of us, here and now, with his body of love. This union of love he achieves in the sacrament of forgiveness and reconciliation. In this sacrament, he comes to us today with his embrace of forgiveness, erasing time and space, to say, "I absolve you; I embrace you." How beautiful to examine these two sacraments—Eucharist and reconciliation—through which Jesus seeks to be present and to give his body of love to us. This is what Jesus seeks with each of us through the Eucharist: to annul time and space and to be married to us as we pass through the hours and days of our earthly lives. As he did through the supreme and extraordinary gift of his body, so he wants us to make concrete and tangible the experience of forgiveness as we live the sacrament of marriage.

As any married couple knows, forgiveness is essential and cannot be taken for granted. For forgiveness to be real, we must feel it deep within ourselves. Just as in the Eucharist Jesus gives physical expression to his love, so in the sacrament of reconciliation we feel his embrace.

Through the sacrament of reconciliation we have the possibility of knowing the embrace of the merciful Father toward the prodigal son. But this is not just a story from the Bible or even only the story between each person and God. It is also a story of our family when our child no longer believes in the love of the Father. When love within the family is poor or is lived superficially, the sense of alienation toward one another deepens this poverty. In the end, this poverty results in self-justification ("But what do you want to do? I cannot do more! What can I expect from him or her?")

Only by contemplating the concrete and infinite love of Eucharist can we come to understand the greatness of the love the Lord offers through the sacrament of forgiveness. It is through the body given for love that Jesus comes to us and embraces us with his mercy.

Celebrating forgiveness is enjoying the faithfulness of Jesus who, by his very nature, is unable to abandon or betray us in the marriage he has created. What a great comfort it is to know this: Jesus will never leave us. In the sacrament of reconciliation, he communicates to each of us individually his faithfulness.

Nothing, no sin, can make him break the marriage bond that he gives us in the Eucharist, and that, in our poverty, we respond to with our very small *amen*. For us, that amen is enough. When we receive the body of Jesus, he, Jesus, Son of God, is bound to us in an eternal and unfailing love.

Observe how the church in its wisdom, aware of what the Eucharist is, starts every celebration with a penitential rite. Often we do not fully understand the meaning, but it is beautiful: "I confess to almighty God, and to you, my brothers and sisters, that I have sinned . . ."[2] This is a sign that Eucharist is already in our hearts even before we even receive it, because only in looking at that Eucharist do we understand how far away our hearts and souls are from the love of Jesus.

It is through this love, which begins in Jesus and lives in our hearts, that we become aware of forgiveness and are able to listen to the Word. Notice the sequence: after confessing my sins, because I have realized the greatness of Jesus' love, I am ready to listen to his Word and engage in the liturgy.

Asking the Father's mercy and celebrating it in the name of Jesus through confession is recognition of how Jesus' love helps us to confess. He brings us to confession, hears our confession, and embraces us in reconciliation. This is his all-encompassing love.

It is only this great forgiveness—endless and unbroken—that leads us to celebrate the liturgy of forgiveness in our marriages and families. Any lesser motivation is mere politeness and excuse-making. Apologies and excuses are certainly important; indeed, they are beautiful, significant for interpersonal relations, and a sign of a good education and a refined humanity. But they are not the focus of the liturgy.

The great loving liturgy of Jesus in the Eucharist, in the sacrament of reconciliation, constantly renews the disciple's relationship with the Lord and teaches us how to celebrate the liturgy of forgiveness in married and family life. Without it, forgiveness becomes a kind of score-keeping between the spouses, who track their own and the other's faults and mistakes. Without it, justice replaces love at the center of the marriage relationship: each spouse takes a place of judgment over the other and demands justice. With this false understanding of forgiveness, it is possible for couples to unconsciously feel a sense of revenge: "Just wait. I will get my turn." This is not forgiveness, but a tenuous agreement that permits even small mistakes to create feelings of betrayal.

We must always remember that the source of both love and forgiveness is Jesus. No other authentic source is possible, especially within a Christian marriage. We can be taught and learn many things in a circumstance, but teaching and learning alone are insufficient. We need God's power to love and forgive.

ASKED FORGIVENESS

To ask forgiveness is always the sign of a turnaround. It is more important than an apology. To ask forgiveness is to admit we have missed a sign of love. To ask forgiveness is to acknowledge that we have missed the opportunity to love. By taking the initiative in asking for forgiveness, we trigger the greatness of the love that comes from God—not from human calculation that seeks to coerce an apology from the other. After having seen and experienced the love of Jesus, the desire and need to ask for forgiveness springs within us.

Seeking forgiveness comes from the awareness of the love that we have received from God and from the person we have offended. If we do not begin with the love of God, we will not have the strength and perspective we need to truly forgive. To ask for forgiveness is first to reorient our heart to the Lord, even before we turn to our husband or wife.

If our hearts to do not move toward the Lord before we ask forgiveness from our spouse, we risk a false forgiveness, a manifestation of our psychology rather than a true forgiveness for the sake of love. Such a confession cannot have the blessing of the Lord.

To ask forgiveness is to welcome the grace of God and to retrace our steps. Through grace, we are given a new heart and new understanding that takes away the veil of pride, because it directs our attention to Jesus who, without sin, covered himself with our sins and redeemed them by his greater love.

To ask for forgiveness, we are helped to descend the staircase of our pride. In this light, the forgiveness sought is an echo, continuity, and preparation for the sacramental forgiveness celebrated in the sacrament of confession and the corporate plea for forgiveness asked at each Mass. Every Sunday we pronounce: "I confess to almighty God, and to you, my brothers and sisters, that I have sinned in thought, word, deed, and omission."[3] But if this confession is never made between the spouses, what value can this formula have? Sins are not made in heaven, but on earth, in our most intimate relationships with one another. If we do not recognize this, our confession becomes nothing but powerless words. Unless we go back to the source of confession and reconciliation—the love of God—we understand neither our sin nor the forgiveness we receive.

If we want to know whether the confession is real, we can look to our behavior in the week preceding and following confession, as well as at the moment we make it. It is in the home and within the family that forgiveness is given and received. What we celebrate in the confessional and the Mass must be consistent with what happens in our lives every other day of the week.

In asking for forgiveness, we are being formed as a couple and as a family in our consciences and our ability to comprehend our sin. Every personal sin mars and distorts our married and family life. When we ask for forgiveness, we are letting ourselves be forgiven; understanding and acting out our need for love; and preparing to receive that love. In letting ourselves be forgiven, we are also forgiving as we give and receive love from God and one another.

FORGIVING

Forgiving is celebrating the signs of love. It is like the embrace of a mother for a child who has suffered a serious injury. She throws herself on the torn body of the child, and no blood or ugliness can stop her. This is forgiveness: it embraces the spouse, though scarred and disfigured by sin. Forgiveness reveals the true power of the love we have received in Jesus.

Forgiveness is the other side of the coin of the great mystery. Spouses participate in the merciful love of Christ for the church; hence they are enabled to love one another as Christ has loved us.[4] Mercy is forgiveness embodied in the extreme loneliness of the cross, forgiveness without being understood. This is the grace the bride and groom receive. Forgiving makes this source of love pour forth, a source of forgiveness that is in the couple just because they are married. Forgiving is to allow that living water to pour out from a source of mercy that is in the spouses and allows them to see everything through the eyes of Jesus, with his merciful love present among them. The truth of my wife is how the merciful Jesus sees her. The truth of my husband is how the merciful Jesus sees him. Everything else is only the surface of the grace of the sacrament of marriage.

The spouses partake of the mercy of Jesus to his community-bride, given through his body. Forgiveness takes the heart of stone and returns the heart of flesh. Forgiveness ends the tallying of committed wrongs, which, no matter how severe, are never an excuse to give a love that does not reflect that of Jesus. How many times the received wrongs are pampered and even savored. Would that we gave this attention instead to the spouse who has sinned rather than wallow in self-pity!

Removing the hardened heart brings the bride and groom out from this quagmire of self-pity and lets them enter the sight of God. However, the forgiveness a couple exchanges is never just one word. We must practice our liturgy over and over with a smile, a hug. We must practice it by speaking to our spouse with love and respect before others.

Forgiveness is the measure by which we will be measured: "Our Father, forgive me as I forgive." This means that when we fail to forgive—to act upon the forgiveness the Lord has given to us—we risk writing our own condemnation. Forgiveness does not grow in a moment, but neither can it be postponed. It should be built, step-by-step, beginning with prayer for the spouse who forgives or asks for forgiveness, even up to the greatest forgiveness, when the thing being forgiven is betrayal.

Forgiveness is the highest gift. We are called to give our body even up to death. But there is also the gift of the soul, even up to welcoming and receiving the deadly wound—betrayal—while remaining ready to love. This is what Jesus did at the Last Supper.

In the eyes of the world this is weakness or naivety, but in the eyes of God it means actualizing here and now, the love of Jesus for each of us. Someone must shout this love to the world. Someone must tell the world of a love that is always and everywhere faithful, like that of Jesus who never leaves us and never will leave us until, in this world, with our last breath, we whisper: "Yes, I still love you." As long as we breathe, we still have a chance, even if only with the thought, to say to Jesus: "I love you."

Forgiveness is the gift of gifts, the one Jesus came to offer us and that he has especially celebrated in a home. In the story of the paralytic who was lowered from the roof, the man does not ask for and, at first, does not receive a miracle of physical healing (see Mark 2:1–12). Instead, he receives Jesus' greatest gift: "Your sins are forgiven," which is like saying, "You are new; you are the best of yourself." This extraordinary miracle was done in the heart of a home.

Not forgiving in marriage and family life is anti-evangelical, because reconciliation is the heart of evangelization and gives hope to humanity. The absence of forgiveness is always a little divorce. Without the ability to forgive, we are not ready for heaven but only for purgatory until our hearts can freely say: "I love you; I forgive you!" Heaven is the place of the complete wedding, of total fraternity, where all must be fit for the unity of God's love. That unity that we do not build here, we will have to build "over there."

The sacrament of forgiveness—well-celebrated, making us aware of our sins, and helping us deeply experience the mercy of the Lord—enables us to open our hearts to be merciful. This awareness also shows us our sins by teaching us forgiveness in and through our families. The frequent exercise of the liturgy of forgiveness in the couple and family, even for small things, encourages us in spiritual growth. In marriage and family, we cannot avoid a confrontation with our sin and the need to ask, receive, and give forgiveness, and to enjoy again the embrace of the Father. Through our family, we all have the chance to taste the goodness of his love.

Chapter 6

THE ANOINTING OF THE SICK

and

THE LITURGY OF THE FAMILY

The Lord Jesus Christ is at the heart of liturgy. It is Jesus who, through his body, the church, acts in the liturgy. It is with and in him that our praise and giving glory rise to God, and from him that salvation manifests itself to us. Jesus baptizes. It is he who gives his Spirit in confirmation, makes himself present in the Eucharist, and gives reconciliation.

The same is true for the anointing of sick. In healing, Jesus acts through signs, including that of the priesthood. In the anointing of the sick, Jesus cares for those who suffer in their bodies and sustains, heals, and raises them to health and life.

James instructs us:

> Is anyone among you sick? He should summon the presbyters of the church, and they should pray over him and anoint [him] with oil in the name of the Lord, and the prayer of

faith will save the sick person, and the Lord will raise him up. If
he has committed any sins, he will be forgiven. (James 5:14–15)

This connection between physical and spiritual healing is crit-
ical. As the *Catechism* recalls:

From ancient times in the liturgical traditions of both East and
West, we have testimonies to the practice of anointing of the sick
with blessed oil. Over the centuries the Anointing of the Sick was
conferred more and more exclusively on those at the point of
death. Because of this it received the name "Extreme Unction."
Notwithstanding this evolution the liturgy has never failed to beg
the Lord that the sick person may recover his health if it would
be conducive to his salvation.[1]

The Second Vatican Council restores light and clarity to this
sacrament. In *Lumen gentium* we read:

By the sacred anointing of the sick and the prayer of her priests the
whole Church commends the sick to the suffering and glorified
Lord, asking that He may lighten their suffering and save them;
she exhorts them, moreover, to contribute to the welfare of the
whole people of God by associating themselves freely with the
passion and death of Christ.[2]

The *Catechism* deepens our understanding. First we deal with
the problem of the illness and the attitude of the sick person
before God. The man of the Old Testament lives his sickness in
the presence of God. It is before God that he laments his illness,
and it is of God, Master of life and death, that he implores healing.
Illness becomes a way to conversion; God's forgiveness initiates the
healing. It is the experience of Israel that illness is mysteriously
linked to sin and evil, and that faithfulness to God according to his
law restores life: "For I, the LORD, am your healer" (Exod. 15:26).
The prophet Isaiah intuits that suffering can also have a redemptive meaning for the sins of others (see Isaiah 53:11). Finally, Isaiah

announces that God will usher in a time for Zion when he will pardon every offense and heal every illness (see Isaiah 33:24).

In illness, the compassion of Jesus is radically manifested: Christ's compassion toward the sick and his many healings of every kind of infirmity are a resplendent sign that "God has visited his people" and that the kingdom of God is close at hand. Jesus has the power not only to heal, but also to forgive sins; he has come to heal the whole man, soul and body; he is the Physician the sick have need of; his compassion toward all who suffer goes so far that he identifies himself with them: "I was sick and you visited me" (Matt. 25:36 ESV). His preferential love for the sick has not ceased through the centuries to draw the very special attention of Christians toward all those who suffer in body and soul. It is the source of tireless efforts to comfort them.[3]

Attention to the sick has always been a key part of the church's witness to the world. Through medical missions, especially in impoverished countries, the church has cared for the sick and sought to heal every kind of suffering. Christian leaders, priests, and nuns have founded hospitals and nursing homes that have relieved the suffering of millions around the world. These acts of mercy all grow from the love of Jesus and his concern for the sick. But this concern for the sick also needs to be our concern, whether we work directly with the physically ill or indirectly through and with our families, wherever we find illness.

Jesus gave us a very clear and strong example: often Jesus asks the sick to believe. He makes use of signs to heal: spittle and the laying on of hands, mud and washing. The sick try to touch him, "because power came forth from him and healed them all" (Luke 6:19). And so, in the sacraments Christ continues to "touch" us in order to heal us.[4]

The sacramental signs of healing are the means by which Jesus continues to draw us near. In the sacrament of the anointing of the sick, it is Jesus who acts, bringing comfort and healing to the sick. Moved by so much suffering, Christ not only allows himself to be touched by the sick, but he makes their miseries his own:

"He took our illnesses and bore our diseases" (Matt. 8:17 ESV; cf. Isaiah 53:4). But he did not heal all the sick. His healings were signs of the coming of the kingdom of God. They announced a more radical healing: the victory over sin and death through his Passover.[5]

We must always remember that the family is called to accompany the sick. Jesus healed diseases as a sign that he had power to bring more intimate, deeper healing. Think for a moment about how many times Jesus, after healing someone, commanded him not to say anything to anyone. He did not want to be mistaken as only a healer and to draw attention to the outward signs of his power. The true power of Jesus is that which heals the deepest evil, the evil of the world and the soul. The *Catechism* states: "By his passion and death on the cross Christ has given a new meaning to suffering: it can henceforth configure us to him and unite us with his redemptive Passion."[6]

Jesus practiced works of healing and directed his disciples to carry on his work among the sick. Christ invites his disciples to follow him by taking up their cross in their turn. By following him they acquire a new outlook on illness and the sick. Jesus associates them with his own life of poverty and service. He makes them share in his ministry of compassion and healing: "So they went out and proclaimed that people should repent. And they cast out many demons and anointed with oil many that were sick and healed them" (Mark 6:12–13 ESV).[7]

Jesus continues this work after his resurrection and ascension. "The risen Lord renews this mission ('In my name . . . they will lay their hands on the sick, and they will recover' [Mark 16:17–18 ESV]) and confirms it through the signs that the Church performs by invoking his name."[8]

And the Holy Spirit gives to some a "special charism of healing so as to make manifest the power of the grace of the risen Lord. But even the most intense prayers do not always obtain the healing of all illnesses."[9]

Sometimes we feel the dilemma of the unanswered prayer: we ask for healing and yet it does not come. The truth is that Jesus does not come to heal diseases of body and mind. This kind of healing remains a sign of the need for a deeper and more intimate healing and, ultimately, of the need for eternal salvation. Our diseases are another sign of our brokenness and an outward expression of our dire need for Jesus. The *Catechism* continues:

> Thus St. Paul must learn from the Lord that "my grace is sufficient for you, for my power is made perfect in weakness," and that the sufferings to be endured can mean that "in my flesh I complete what is lacking in Christ's afflictions for the sake of his Body, that is the church."[10]

This awareness emerges clearly in the action of the church in favor of the sick: "Heal the sick" (Matt. 10:8 ESV). The church has received this charge from the Lord and strives to carry it out by taking care of the sick as well as by accompanying them with her prayer of intercession. She believes in the life-giving presence of Christ, the Physician of souls and bodies. This presence is particularly active through the sacraments, and in an altogether special way through the Eucharist, the bread that gives eternal life and that St. Paul suggests is connected with bodily health.[11]

THE EFFECTS OF ANOINTING THE SICK

The *Catechism* teaches that the anointing of the sick is "a special gift of the Holy Spirit":[12]

> The first grace of this sacrament is one of strengthening, peace, and courage to overcome the difficulties that go with the condition of serious illness or the frailty of old age. This grace is a gift of the Holy Spirit, who renews trust and faith in God and strengthens against the temptations of the evil one, the temptation to discouragement and anguish in the face of death. This assistance from the Lord by the power of his Spirit is meant to lead the sick person

to healing of the soul, and also of the body if such is God's will. Furthermore, "if he has committed sins, he will be forgiven."[13]

These passages are astonishingly beautiful. Jesus makes himself close through the gift of the Spirit, giving what is most important at the moment of extreme suffering: peace; courage; and the strength to overcome difficulties, renew confidence and faith in God, and avoid the temptation of discouragement and anguish before death. Through this sacrament, Jesus especially wants to bring the sick to the conscious understanding of the soul being healed and turned to God.

Next, we see the way anointing brings the ill person into union with the passion of Christ:

> By the grace of this sacrament the sick person receives the strength and the gift of uniting himself more closely to Christ's Passion: in a certain way he is consecrated to bear fruit by configuration to the Savior's redemptive Passion. Suffering, a consequence of original sin, acquires a new meaning: it becomes a participation in the saving work of Jesus.[14]

The crucified and resurrected Jesus is present in the sacrament of the anointing, and in this sacrament he carries the marks of the crucifixion. He is risen; he is alive; his wounds are glorious. He stands beside the sick person and unites his or her suffering to his own, thereby ennobling and suffusing with meaning the human suffering he visits. Such suffering is not lost or wasted because Jesus joins our suffering to his. By the power of Jesus, our suffering becomes part of his saving work.

The church also benefits from the sacrament of anointing. The sick who receive this sacrament, "by freely uniting themselves to the passion and death of Christ," contribute to the "good of the people of God."[15] "By celebrating this sacrament the church, in the communion of saints, intercedes for the benefit of the sick person, and he, for his part, through the grace of this sacrament, contributes to the sanctification of the church and to the good of all men for whom the church suffers and offers herself through Christ to God the Father."[16]

By living faithfully in illness, we make a living sacrifice to the church. The world often sees the sick as dead weight, an obstruction to the fulfillment of our own lives. For Christians, the opposite is true. The greater the suffering experienced in Jesus, the more it becomes a gift for the whole church. The sufferer becomes a person who lives more intimately in the passion of Jesus and in his grace.

And finally, the sacrament of anointing of the sick is preparation for the final journey:

> If the sacrament of anointing the sick is given to all who suffer from serious illness and infirmity, even more rightly it is given to those at the point of departing this life; so it is also called *sacramentum exeuntium* [the sacrament of those departing]. The anointing of the sick completes our conformity to the death and resurrection of Christ, just as Baptism began it. It completes the holy anointings that mark the whole Christian life: that of Baptism which sealed the new life in us, and that of Confirmation which strengthened us for the combat of this life. This last anointing fortifies the end of our earthly life like a solid rampart for the final struggles before entering the Father's house.[17]

How, then, is the anointing of the sick expressed in and through the domestic church of marriage and family?

FROM THE LITURGY OF THE CHURCH TO THE LITURGY OF THE FAMILY

Through the sacrament of marriage, Christ the Lord links his presence to the newlyweds: he is with them and "remains with them" throughout their lives.[18] The Lord asks them to be a living sacrament of his presence of love for humanity and for the church.

To be able to see the sacrament of the anointing of the sick with new eyes and understand its expression in family life, we need to start from the grace of marriage. A married couple lives and is a sign of the presence of Jesus and his love. In and through the spouses, Christ seeks to love every person.

The Jesus who lives with the spouses is the resurrected Jesus, the one who sits at the right hand of the Father. This Jesus makes himself one with their married life and accompanies them toward their final and definitive union with the Creator.

At the same time, in their marriage and as parents, spouses know the origin and destiny of every life. The bride and groom ponder the mystery of each other's beginning. If they are blessed with children, they experience the wonder of bringing new life into the world and pondering the future of this life. The Christian couple knows that every life comes from God and is destined toward the fullness of love in God.

So what is the relationship between the sacrament of marriage and sacrament of the anointing of the sick, and how is it celebrated in marriage and family?

CELEBRATION OF LIFE

The married couple and family live a celebration of life as they give praise to the Father in the Holy Spirit for each life, and at the same time ask for salvation—the fullness of life—for everyone. In Psalm 139 we read: "I praise you, because I am wonderfully made" (v. 14).

Spouses celebrate life in conception, throughout pregnancy, in childbirth, and in raising a child. They also celebrate life by remaining beside each other and by knowing the origin, destiny, and beauty of the other. Faith in the God of life, who created every man and woman, gives us a new way to look at him. In *Evangelium Vitae*, Saint John Paul II affirms this:

> We need first to foster . . . a contemplative outlook. It is the outlook of those who see life in its deeper meaning, who grasp its utter gratuitousness, its beauty. . . . It is the outlook of those who do

> not presume to take possession of reality but instead accept it as
> a gift, discovering . . . in every person his living. This outlook
> does not give in to discouragement when confronted by those
> who are sick, suffering, outcast or at death's door. Instead, in all
> these situations it feels challenged.[19]

It is here that we capture the deep meaning of the anointing of the sick. It is Jesus who approaches the ill person because he wants to stay next to every person throughout his or her life. In a special way, he makes himself present through the sacrament of the anointing in the time of sickness, suffering, or departure from this life. The bride and groom, in their unique triune relationship with the Holy Spirit, are the celebrants of life from beginning to end. Through the most common activities of life—cooking, cleaning, working—the couple celebrates and communicates a life that is always directed toward God. We will never be able to understand fully the strength and beauty of Jesus, who makes himself present in the time of sickness, without understanding that he makes himself present through the spouses in every moment of life.

Spouses are priests of life. The spouses create new life when they are joined in a one-flesh union by the sacrament of marriage; they transmit life in the creation and nurture of children; and they express life to the broader community. Because the one-flesh union uniquely expresses divine and human life across the entire lifespan, the spouses have a unique understanding of suffering, illness, and departure from this life. Through the priestly office of marriage, the anointing of the sick shows us that we cannot truly care for the sick if we are not attentive to life at every other point of its development. This perspective permits real care and service to the sick because we can see that the source of life is also its destiny.

The life of our wife or child or neighbor comes from God and is meant for God. Our purpose is to celebrate the life given and to thank Jesus for it. We often experience times when our physical presence is the only comfort we can give the ill. In these moments, we must turn to Jesus to act as celebrant of life, and to bring the inner healing we are unable to give. The married couple, in its manifestation of God's life, can help bring this presence of Jesus to the sick.

BESIDE THE SUFFERING LIFE

In this context of the celebration of life, we also find all the moments, short or long, in which life is susceptible to disease, suffering, and death. In fact, though, these situations have a deep meaning of proclamation of God's love.

In a society that values and classifies people according to their efficiency, productivity, or other economic value, the knowledge of the fragility and impermanence of life becomes precious. A false sense of control and conquest leads us to believe that we possess life and may dispose of it at will.

Illness and suffering have always been among the hardest problems of human life. Our contemporary culture regards disease, especially serious illness, as only a reminder of death. In such illness, man experiences his own powerlessness, limitation, and finitude. Illness can lead to anguish, alienation, despair, and rebellion against God. For the Christian, however, disease and illness become an opportunity to meditate on and understand our destiny. Deep within us, we understand that we are made for joy and fullness of life, not suffering. Suffering is something that must be overcome so that joy and fulfillment can occur. This transforms moments of suffering into an extraordinary opportunity to proclaim the gospel of life to the world. It can also make us more mature, helping us to discern the trivial from the essential. Very often, we find in illness the opportunity to redirect our life toward God.

To celebrate life is not to make it an absolute value, but to place it in the perspective of its origin and its destiny. With illness and suffering, we discover that earthly life does not explain the instinct for survival, peace, fulfillment, and joy—much less our desire for eternity. Eternity calls to us, and these instincts are the response of our souls to that call.

A mother who is dying, or a father who sees a dying son, shouts this in grief to the world. The passion of a lover, or of a husband or a wife who is leaving proclaims this. Illness and death are deep wounds to our instinct for eternity and our need for continuity. Spouses, who have grown in unity over many years, are teachers of eternity. Day-by-day they build their marriage in preparation of the definitive marriage with God. The special presence of the Holy Spirit in marriage gives spouses the key to understanding that illness and death violate our desire for union and continuity with pain and sorrow, and that this violation is a sign that we are intended for eternity. Any effort to find these satisfactions in this life cannot succeed.

Further, the spouses, who intuit the definitive marriage that awaits them, draw close to each person in an attitude of care. They show the suffering person, here and now, the love that will bless them in heaven.

These ideas describe an ideal that is very far from the situations many people experience, even among church-going Christians. Many times, the sacrament of the anointing of the sick is not requested. Priests are no longer called, even in situations of serious illness, because the sick have been denied the knowledge of impending death. This kind of denial or deception deprives the seriously ill of the most important blessing and comfort they can receive. The anointing of the sick is an opportunity to understand the last moments of life in awareness of the beauty of faith, and it gives us the chance to say, "I'm coming to meet you, Lord."

We do not care for life only when it is healthy and does not impose a burden on us. We care for life because that life gives glory to God and because we can help prepare that person and ourselves to give full and ultimate praise. The care we give helps the sick to taste the love of their brothers and sisters; to enter into praise and thanksgiving as part of their earthly community; and to prepare for their passage into the presence of eternal love.

Contemporary culture has, in many ways, deprived us of the ability to interpret life in the light of ultimate things. We forget that we are made for eternal life. Illness helps us to open ourselves to the afterlife, instead of becoming only a burden that imposes vast costs, personal and financial, as we seek physical healing. Many focus excessively on health, constantly seeking after new cures because health and staying alive is, in this view, more precious than heaven. In married couples, it is Christ who acts as a presence of love, stands close to each sick person, and shows him the way to his destiny.

As Christians, we never hope to die before God wills us to do so even if there are times when, in our suffering, we might desire heaven. Paul, finding himself in a particular situation, said: "I desire to be with the Lord."[20] But these are moments of trial and difficulty, in which circumstances temporarily undermine our will to live. Nevertheless, we are called to live life to the fullest because every moment allows us to express a possibility of love; every moment of life is an opportunity to grow in maturity and open our hearts more because we know now in part—and one day will fully know—the Lord.

In this perspective, spouses may become protagonists in the anointing of the sick. The bride and groom know they are the church, the domestic church. They experience the presence of Jesus, but they also know that their life does not exhaust the mystery of Jesus' love. The love of Jesus for humanity and for the church does not end in the sacrament of a couple, and not even in all the sacraments of marriage. The action of Jesus is infinitely beyond us, beyond our ministry, and beyond the priesthood of all believers. The fullness of God's ministry to the world can only be known through communion with the whole church.

Spouses' special awareness of Jesus' presence in their marriage, together with their understanding of the full journey of life to the final marriage, is why husband and wife together proclaim and promote the anointing of the sick. They are able to speak to the origin and destiny of each person, because they have experienced and contemplated each step of life. Through the sacrament of anointing, they can propose interior healing, regardless of the severity of the illness and suffering, which helps the sick person to a deeper and more intimate communion with the Lord.

May the Lord help all married couples to live more intensely their own call to the eternal wedding and to be the priests of life. In doing so, they provide an opportunity to others to prepare deeply, interiorly, for our final destiny, our definitive wedding with the Lord.

Chapter 7

THE LITURGY OF THE WORD IN THE FAMILY

THE CENTRALITY OF THE WORD

The Word of God is a central concern of the Christian life. In *Verbum Domini,* Pope Benedict XVI explains:

> The relationship between Christ, the Word of the Father, and the Church cannot be fully understood in terms of a mere past event; rather, it is a living relationship which each member of the faithful is personally called to enter into. We are speaking of the presence of God's word to us today: "Lo, I am with you always, to the close of the age."[1]

In a unique way, Jesus becomes a contemporary of all humanity in every age through the Word. Through the Word we hear the voice of Jesus speaking to us today. *Dei Verbum* expresses this mystery as a nuptial dialogue:

> God, who spoke of old, uninterruptedly converses with the bride of His beloved Son; and the Holy Spirit, through whom the living voice of the Gospel resounds in the Church, and

through her, in the world, leads unto all truth those who believe and makes the word of Christ dwell abundantly in them.[2]

In Jesus Christ, the Word that God addressed to humanity becomes flesh with us; the invisible God, out of the abundance of his love, speaks to men as friends and lives among them so that he may invite and take them into fellowship with himself.[3]

The Word enables us to live in communion with God. Unfortunately, we often do not enter well and completely into the great gift we have been given in the Word.

> Then, after speaking in many and varied ways through the prophets, "now at last in these days God has spoken to us in His Son." For He sent His Son, the eternal Word, who enlightens all men, so that He might dwell among men and tell them of the innermost being of God. Jesus Christ, therefore, the Word made flesh, was sent as "a man to men." He "speaks the words of God," and completes the work of salvation which His Father gave Him to do.[4]

We cannot and must never try to detach the Word from the living Jesus, nor detach the living Jesus from the Word. They are intrinsically united: Jesus is the Word made flesh, and his flesh tells us the Word of God. If we detach the Word from Jesus, then the Christian faith becomes the religion of the book, and we lose the identity of our faith. The written Word reaches our thoughts and causes us to reflect. But if it does not enter our hearts and souls, it can also produce an ideology. If we detach the living Jesus from the Word, we no longer have the risen Jesus. He becomes instead a historical figure—not the risen Savior we need to join us individually and in the church. For, the Word made flesh is the Jesus who leads me to the Father in the power of the Holy Spirit.

The Word is the train on which I can go to God at any moment. The Word is the train that comes from God for me at every moment. It is not surprising that Benedict XVI emphasizes the "sacramentality of the Word":

> Here it may help to recall that Pope John Paul II had made reference to the "sacramental character of revelation" and in particular to "the sign of the Eucharist in which the indissoluble unity between the signifier and signified makes it possible to grasp the depths of the mystery." We come to see that at the heart of the sacramentality of the word of God is the mystery of the Incarnation itself: "the Word became flesh," the reality of the revealed mystery is offered to us in the "flesh" of the Son.[5]

The sacramentality of the Word of God is the mystery of the incarnation: "The Word was made flesh." The reality of the revealed mystery of incarnation is offered to us in the resurrected flesh of the Son. The Word of God is offered to us in the flesh of the Son and becomes perceptible to us through the words and actions of Jesus. Our faith, therefore, recognizes the Word of God, and we welcome the signs and words with which Jesus comes to us. The more we welcome the Word, the more we welcome the Son of God made flesh. Not welcoming the Word means rejecting the Word of God made flesh. The sacramentality of the Word can thus be understood in analogy to the real presence of Christ in the Eucharist. By approaching the altar and taking part in the eucharistic banquet, we communicate with the body and blood of Jesus, the Word of God made flesh.

The proclamation of the Word of God in the celebration implies our recognition that Christ himself is present and welcoming us. To take the Eucharist without accepting his Word is a contradiction, because Jesus is present in his Word. The Liturgy of the Word that is proclaimed before the consecration is the Word of God that urges us to wake up and accept Jesus.

THE WORD PROCLAIMED IN THE LITURGY AND IN THE CHURCH

The church is the guardian of the Word: "In considering the Church as 'the home of the Word,' attention must first be given to the sacred liturgy, for the liturgy is the privileged setting in which God speaks to us in the midst of our lives . . ."[6]

The church is the "home of the Word" where God seeks us out and speaks to us. Scripture is not a history book that only describes events of the past. Through it, God speaks to his people today, who listen and respond. In this response, the Word is fulfilled for us.

Every liturgical act is, by its nature, full of the Holy Scripture. As stated in *Sacrosanctum Concilium*:

> Sacred scripture is of the greatest importance in the celebration of the liturgy. For it is from scripture that lessons are read and explained in the homily, and psalms are sung; the prayers, collects, and liturgical songs are scriptural in their inspiration and their force, and it is from the scriptures that actions and signs derive their meaning.[7]

Verbum Domini also tells us: even more, it must be said that Christ himself "is present in his word, since it is he who speaks when Scripture is read in Church."[8] Listening to the Word and truly hearing it is essential preparation for receiving the Eucharist.

Indeed, the liturgical celebration becomes a continuous, complete, and effective proclamation of the Word of God. The Word of God, proclaimed without ceasing in the liturgy of the church, is always alive and active. The liturgy expresses the power of the Holy Spirit, and it manifests the Father's love, which never ceases to do good for all people. From its inception, the church has been aware that the Word of God in the liturgy is accompanied by the intimate action of the Holy Spirit, who makes it alive in the hearts of his people. In *Verbum Domini*, we find:

> Thanks to the Paraclete, "the word of God becomes the foundation of the liturgical celebration, and the rule and support of all our life. The working of the same Holy Spirit . . . brings home to each person individually everything that in the proclamation of the word of God is spoken for the good of the whole gathering. In strengthening the unity of all, the Holy Spirit at the same

time fosters a diversity of gifts and furthers their multiform operation."[9]

The same proclaimed Word often has different echoes depending on the person who listens to it. Sometimes, even husband and wife—listening to the same Word—receive different emphases when listening. This is because the Holy Spirit is always the "simultaneous interpreter" and "customizer" of the Word. Through the Holy Spirit, the Word penetrates deeply and uniquely the heart of each person.

THE WORD IN FAMILY LIFE

Meditating on the meaning of the Word and its place in family life, we are discussing neither mere intellectualism, nor an inquiry into the written meaning of the Word, nor the cultural significance of the Word in the family. For the Holy Scriptures are not just a book on a shelf. Instead, our aim is to examine how the family can build a living, vital, and essential relationship with the Word, because the Word himself lives in and through the relationship of the married couple.

THE WORD AS ORIGIN AND FOUNDATION OF MARRIAGE

The Word supplies the source and meaning of marriage for anyone who seeks to understand it. *Verbum Domini* tells us:

> With the proclamation of the Word of God, the Church reveals to Christian families their true identity, what it is and what it must be in accordance with the Lord's plan (*Familiaris Consortio*, 49). Consequently, it must never be forgotten that the Word of God is at the very origin of marriage (Genesis 2:24) and that Jesus himself made marriage one of the institutions of his

Kingdom (Matthew 19:4–8), elevating to the dignity of a sacrament what was inscribed in human nature from the beginning. "In the celebration of the sacrament, a man and a woman speak a prophetic word of reciprocal self-giving, that of being 'one flesh,' a sign of the mystery of the union of Christ with the Church (Ephesians 5:31–32)." . . . In the face of widespread confusion in the sphere of affectivity, and the rise of ways of thinking which trivialize the human body and sexual differentiation, the Word of God re-affirms the original goodness of the human being, created as man and woman and called to a love which is faithful, reciprocal and fruitful.[10]

Therefore, the Word rests at the center of a couple and family's identity and provides a precise and unchangeable reference point. This identity never fades or ages. Time and events subtract nothing from the eternal youth of a couple consecrated in the Lord, who with the Holy Spirit, form a new person in one-flesh unity. This triune identity creates a wedding portrait of the couple, with the beauty God conceived in them. For God, no couple gets older or exhausts the beauty of its origin and life in him. Two spouses might be tired, exhausted, and disappointed with one another, but their one-flesh union never changes before God. This couple has the same mission and fruitfulness from its beginning to its parting at death: to proclaim Christ and the church. This timelessness arises precisely from its continuous and permanent origin the living Word of God.

THE WORD MAKES JESUS KNOWN TO THE COUPLE

The Word, Christ the Bridegroom, is known to the couple and leads them into an intimate relationship with him. For, through the sacrament of marriage the couple establishes a deep and indissoluble bond with Bridegroom Jesus. The Second Vatican Council, in *Gaudium et Spes,* tells us that, "Christ the Lord comes into the lives of married Christians through the sacrament of matrimony and abides with them."[11] Spouses, with and in Jesus, are called to re-actualize the loving gift of the Word of God to humanity and the love of Christ for the church. It is the Word itself that enables them to know and understand this great mystery of the love of God.

Spouses are called to reenact the love of God through human flesh. Through their own incarnation they are to reenact the love of Christ for the church. To do so, they must learn the part. But where can they learn it?

The Word accompanies the couple, step-by-step, as they discover the value of their engagement, not as a matter of the past, but as a matter to be lived today. Holy Scripture tells us, "I will betroth you to me forever" (Hos. 2:21); "I will bring you into the desert, I will speak to your heart, I will marry you" (Hos. 2:14); and, "As a young man marries a virgin, your Builder shall marry you" (Isa. 62:5).

Indeed, in the Word of God we find the whole engagement of God to his people. The spouses are called to actualize this engagement, to give voice to this amazing love that teaches the love of God. He desires spouses to relive his love; through this reliving he seeks out his people. God wants us to know that he is in love with us and desires union with us today, just as he desired union with the people of Israel. Bearing witness to this truth is the mission inscribed in the very bodies of a married couple. Spouses who do not understand this mission are a "buried talent," a "lost coin," or a "fountain sealed."[12] Without this knowledge, the abundant life he seeks to give to the entire world is sealed within itself.

Through the married couple, the Lord wants to show to us the patience he manifested in the prophets, so that he can say again: "You are my people, I am your God" (Ezek. 36:24–28). In his patience to meet his beloved community-bride, he sent prophets to Israel, again and again, to make it clear that he is the Lover. Married couples must repeat to the world, through words and actions, that God is love and that God loves his creatures.

Through the Word, the bride and groom become very intimate with the great mystery of the incarnation. In their life together, they live this mystery in their own flesh and bear witness to it with their lives. God loved enough to become one flesh with humanity in the incarnation, and the spouses also experience the love of being one flesh. In the Eucharist, Jesus says: "I have eagerly *desired*" (Luke 22:15–20, emphasis added). This echoes what was already written regarding the incarnation of God, which expressed his passion to join himself to human flesh. It is through the Word that we learn of a God who loves us enough to join us in the flesh in an ordinary family, living a simple life in Nazareth. In our own simple lives, we, too, can live the infinite love of God.

The infinite love can be experienced over a cup of coffee, in a quiet conversation, in the poverty and simplicity of Nazareth. The spouses will be able to understand it only if they know the life of Jesus the Bridegroom. Through the Word, we are able to know the public life of Bridegroom Jesus—how he acts, speaks, and shares his love and life with the whole world. Through the Word, spouses are guided to the peaks of love with Bridegroom Jesus in his death and resurrection. Like Jesus, they will learn to say, "I am willing to lose everything to proclaim the love of God." These are the peaks of love that all Christians live in the Eucharist, and that husband and wife are called to experience and live together.

The Word is, therefore, essential for knowing who Jesus is as spouse. Too many times, spouses have been content only to know a little something of him—things they learned as children—continuing without a deep knowledge of his heart, mind, and actions. In a marriage, this kind of deep knowledge is deeply needed; it is the key to a secure and reciprocal love between husband and wife. In knowing Jesus, this kind of deep knowledge is also necessary. Husband and wife as individuals should know Jesus, and they should also know Jesus together. This knowledge comes to the couple through the Word.

Dei Verbum tells us that "ignorance of the Scriptures is ignorance of Christ."[13] By extension we could say, "Not knowing the Scriptures means not knowing the Bridegroom; not attending to the Word means not knowing the Groom Jesus who lives with the couple."

THE WORD GIVES VOICE TO THE PRESENCE OF JESUS IN COUPLE AND FAMILY LIFE

Knowing Jesus means wanting to know how he sees things and what he thinks. Husbands and wives are always concerned with the thoughts and opinions of their spouses on every question, no matter how small or trivial. Spouses make constant reference to the needs, wishes, and desires of the other. Husband and wife, separately and in their marriage, also need to ask what Jesus thinks. This is the way and pattern of holiness as we attend to the simple and ordinary things of life while seeking the mind and will of Jesus. It is a way that is so simple, it can be achieved by all.

The sacramentality of the Word is understood in analogy to the real presence of Christ in the Eucharist. But the presence of Christ with the spouses is also linked to the sacrament of marriage. Jesus is present with the couple by virtue of the sacrament of marriage, and the family is constituted as a small church, a place of Jesus' presence. Then, what we read in *Sacrosanctum Concilium* can properly be applied also to the family: "Christ is always present in His Church, especially in her liturgical celebrations. . . . He is present in His Word, since it is He Himself who speaks when the Holy Scriptures are read in the Church."[14]

This enables us to say that Christ is always present in the home of a married couple, and he makes himself felt to them especially when they proclaim and listen to the Word. God has given us the Word, which helps us to live in the Trinitarian way of true communication. The Word is given to men and women to build their relationship, up to the highest expression of the nuptial relationship. God has chosen this nuptial word as a vehicle to communicate who he is, what he thinks, and what he wants to say to us and through us to the world.

The Word is the way in which Jesus, present in a home, establishes a relationship, transmits news about himself, and communicates his love for the couple. These things can only happen if we create space for the voice of Jesus to be heard.

The Bible is the concrete way through which the Bridegroom Jesus can speak in a home and be the central figure of the family. He can also do this with a suggestion, a thought, an inspiration that comes from our environment, from a testimony, or from a sermon. But in the home he can only speak as much as the spouses let him through their reading of the Bible. The Holy Spirit strengthens, extends, and energizes the Word to give it the specific meaning it needs to touch the heart of the family and to make its power known and felt.

Therefore, before reading, listening to, and meditating on the Word, it is essential to invoke the Holy Spirit and invite his presence. This same Holy Spirit who attended the bride and groom in the rite of marriage and who actualizes the love of Christ for the church also makes it possible for the Word of Jesus to become effective in the life of the couple.

MAKING IT POSSIBLE FOR JESUS TO SPEAK THROUGH SCRIPTURE

A word, which is external, can only build a relationship with us when we pay attention to it. As we attend to this word, it touches our lives and arrives in our hearts. The same is true of the eternal Word.

Everything that God has given us is stored in the Holy Book, the life of the church. But it will be realized only if we hear it, agree with it, and let it enter our hearts.

The Word is in the book, full of power, waiting for us to read and hear. We can keep the Bible in our homes but if that Word is not read and proclaimed, it will not have space in our hearts to operate. For, the power of the Word is not preserved in the book, but in the hearing, agreeing, and living in the heart of the Word.

LET THE WORD BE PROCLAIMED IN MARRIED AND FAMILY LIFE

We now see, in a very simple way, how the Word can be read and proclaimed. We can approach the Word through personal study. We might read all of the Gospels in sequence or follow the readings of the day proposed by the liturgy in Mass, or in the Breviary. We might linger on some prayers taken from the Word of God—the Our Father, the *Magnificat*, or the Psalmody of Saint Benedict among them. We might even open the Bible randomly and take a passage as a word that the Lord wants to give us.

The couple can also give space to the Word of God together. This is clearly different than personal study. Personal reading of the Bible lets the Word speak to the individual. Husband and wife who study personally can, of course, always share with one another the beauty and the message of that word. But it is a word gained individually. The couple together can experience the Word in all the same ways that the individual can but with the extra dimension of listening to the Word as one flesh. Welcoming the Word as a couple means reading it together and letting Jesus speak to both listeners at the same time. Facing a difficult decision or situation, the couple, through the Word, is able to ask Jesus what he thinks or what he would do. The Word of God embeds itself in their hearts and minds and is recalled to help in facing the challenges of life. In this way, the Word becomes a pathway for the growth of the couple.

Another way to receive the Word is as a couple together with children. This helps the children to center their attention on

Jesus who, for parents, is a living presence and has a living word. It is vital for the education of children that they see their parents believe in the Word and value it above the words of books, newspapers, and television. If the children learn that the Word is a treasure that speaks, then they will seek it in the future as a way of holiness and in times of trouble, solitude, and old age. Therefore, by reading the Word together, the family tries to understand what Jesus wants to say to the family, or to individual family members.

The Word can also be enjoyed in homes when we open the door to friends, acquaintances, neighbors, and relatives. This is part of the extraordinary gift of "building the Church in the home" and allowing Jesus to work through the family into the society around it. Our homes, through the Family Communities for Evangelization[15] and other religious initiatives, become places where people are invited to encounter the living Word of God in Jesus. It could be something as simple and natural as inviting friends to our homes to join as the family reads aloud from the Bible. Through opportunities like this, many people can come to know what the Word can bring to life and that the Word is life.

LET THE WORD BE WELCOMED IN SILENCE

To be a true hearer of the Word, the individual, the couple, and the children must be silent. Hearing the Word is like hearing someone call to us from a distance: we must turn off the radio; ask the children to be quiet; and cup our hand behind our ear to try to hear. There is no other way to hear and understand what is being said. So it is with the Word of God. Jesus is the mysterious traveler who accompanies the disciples on the way to Emmaus. The disciples are only able to hear Jesus when they silence themselves and begin to listen. Likewise, we must learn to try to hear the quiet, far-off voice and move away from our experience, passions, and problems. We have to go to the edge of our existence to understand the voice that comes from beyond the events of our daily lives. Equipped with the wisdom we gain, we are able to find solutions for the day-to-day challenges of life and family.

The Word must be understood in its beauty and its desire to meet us. We must desire the Word both as individuals and as couples. The Word builds the family and helps us reach others through the family, because the family is not an end in itself. As with Abraham, Isaac, and Jacob, the family serves to spread the Word and create disciples so that they might number like grains of sand along the seashore.

LET THE WORD ENTER THE HEART

Just as the Word must reach the heart of the individual to be effective, so the Word must also reach the inner room of the couple.[16] In *Dei Verbum* we read: "Prayer should accompany the reading of Sacred Scripture, so that God and man may talk together; for 'we speak to Him when we pray; we hear Him when we read the divine saying.'"[17]

In the parable of the sower we read: "Unless a grain of wheat falls to the ground and dies, it remains just a grain of wheat" (John 12:24). Jesus tells us: "If you remain [abide] in my word, you will truly be my disciples and you will know the truth, and the truth will set you free" (John 8:31–32).

"Abiding in the Word" is to be at home with the Word. We could say the Word is at home with us. The relationship is between God the Trinity and us. We two become one flesh and are joined to Jesus the Bridegroom. It is certain that the Word comes from the heart of God, by his immense love for each of us. If it comes from the heart of God who also interprets and makes the Word alive, it will more deeply and completely engage the heart of the individual and the one-flesh heart of the couple. It is not the same thing to say to a friend, "I'm expecting a child," as it is to say these words to a husband. The depth of experience shared between husband and wife gives the sentence a different meaning. Likewise, hearing the Word from the Bridegroom Jesus, spoken to the couple he has wed, is the word of love spoken by the Lover.

Marriage gives concrete expression to God's love for humanity and the love of Christ for the church. The Word gives a couple the permanent mission to build the great and extraordinary work that God sees in marriage. We can only see this possibility in marriage with the eyes of faith. Where we see a block of marble, the artist sees the work that will be born from it. The Word, which calls marriage the "great mystery," helps us to see in part the beauty that God has destined the couple to become. No one but God can fully see this beauty, because he has designed it and called it to be made in his image. In the tri-unity of marriage—man, woman, and Holy Spirit in a relationship of mutual self-donation—God sees a reflection of his own triune nature. Through his Word, he is able to mold and shape the beauty he has designed for each couple.

Chapter 8

THE LITURGY OF THE HOURS IN THE FAMILY

The church partakes of the Liturgy of the Hours, or the liturgy of time. Alongside the Liturgy of the Hours for the church is a liturgy of hours for the domestic church, marking and sanctifying the family's time. To properly understand what it means to sanctify time, we begin with one fundamental imperative: the need to be always in prayer.

PRAY WITHOUT CEASING

"Even should [a mother] forget [her infant], I will never forget you" (Isa. 49:15). As a mother precedes a child, begets a child, so God has always wanted us to exist and never forgets us. It is striking to remember that each person's DNA is absolutely different; each of us is a child desired by God, loved individually, and entrusted to a father, mother, brothers, and sisters. After calling us to life, the heavenly Father endlessly calls each of us to that mysterious encounter that is prayer.

The wonder of prayer is revealed beside the well where we come seeking water: "There, Christ comes to meet every human being. It is He who first seeks us and asks us for a drink. Jesus thirsts; his asking arises from the depths of God's desire for us. Whether we realize it or not, prayer is the encounter of God's thirst with ours. God thirsts that we may thirst for Him."[1]

In this passage, we see the Samaritan woman at the well. Our prayer gives space to the presence of God, to the Word, to that love that precedes us. Our prayers are always answered, because he is there before we pray, waiting for us, loving us, speaking to us. Prayer is like waking up from the sleep of loneliness, isolation, and life without God. Prayer is recognizing that the Presence is there, that the Lord is with us. In prayer, we recognize this eternal reality by talking to, invoking, and praising him. This is why Paul instructs us to "pray without ceasing" (1 Thess. 5:17) and to sing "to the Lord in [our] hearts, giving thanks always and for everything in the name of our Lord Jesus Christ to God the Father" (Eph. 5:19–20). Paul also tells us to seek God "with all prayer and supplication, pray[ing] at every opportunity in the Spirit. To that end, be watchful with all perseverance and supplication for all the holy ones" (Eph. 6:18). In the Gospel of Luke, the Lord exhorts us to pray always (see Luke 18:1–8).

God's invitation to pray springs from his love for each of us. Our prayer is a response to that love and an expression of our relationship to him. Prayer becomes a silent meditation to express a love that words can no longer contain.

Prayer is an articulation of a love and acknowledgment of a presence that is there already. The admonitions from Paul and from Jesus to pray without ceasing are rooted in the understanding that the Lord is always with us, lives with us, and loves us. In prayer, we awaken from our loneliness to God's great love.

LINKED WITH THE PRAYER OF CHRIST

Having recalled Jesus' invitation to pray continuously, we now consider how his disciples have tried to respond to it in the history of the church, using the Liturgy of the Hours, that prayer contained in the Breviary, the Divine Office that priests and religious recite. (The laity are well acquainted with two parts of this liturgy, Morning Lauds and Vespers.) The Liturgy of the Hours, a prayer-in-time, has a beautiful and precious link with the prayer of Christ.

The term *Liturgy of the Hours* was first used in 1959 and was subsequently endorsed by the Second Vatican Council.[2] Since that time it has been used in the official documents of the liturgy. It is called *liturgy,* first of all, because it is part of the public ritual of the church and one of the ways the church responds to the presence of Jesus. Through the Liturgy of the Hours, Jesus, who is present in all liturgical actions, has someone who is praying at every moment of every day—monks, priests, nuns, and laity. In this way, the church never stops responding to the presence of Jesus. And, as discussed in chapter 1, through the mystery of Christ this liturgical action, like all others, benefits the entire church—not simply those who are present for it.

The purpose of the Liturgy of the Hours is to sanctify the hours and minutes of the day and night.

> The General Instructions of the Liturgy of the Hours synthetizes this concept: Christ taught us: "You must pray at all times and not lose heart" (Luke 18:1). The church has been faithful in obeying this instruction; it never ceases to offer prayer and makes this exhortation its own: "Through him [Jesus] let us offer to God an unceasing sacrifice of praise" (Heb. 13:15).
>
> The church fulfills this precept not only by celebrating the Eucharist but also by praying through the Liturgy of the Hours. By ancient Christian tradition what distinguishes the Hours from other liturgical services is that it consecrates to God the whole cycle of the day and the night.[3]

The history of the Liturgy of the Hours has its origin in the example and command of Jesus. From the Gospels, we know that prayer was at the heart of the Savior's life. As the *Instructions* tell us:

The Gospels many times show us Christ at prayer: when his mission is revealed by the Father (Luke 3:21–22); before He calls the apostles (Luke 6:12); when He blesses God at the multiplication of the loaves (Matthew 14:19); when He is transfigured on the mountain (Luke 9:28–29); when He heals the deaf-mute (Mark 7:34); raises Lazarus (John 11:41); before He asks for Peter's confession of faith (Luke 9:18); when He teaches the disciples how to pray (Luke 11:1); when the disciples return from their mission (Matthew 11:25); when He blesses the little children (Matthew 19:13); prays for Peter (Luke 22:32); when he would retire into the desert or into the hills to pray (Mark 6:46); rise very early (Mark 1:35); or spend the night up to the fourth watch in prayer to God (Luke 6:12).[4]

This helps us understand how Jesus' constant prayer nurtured his relationship with the Father up to and including his death on the cross: "My God, my God, why have you forsaken me?" (Mark 15:34; see also Luke 23:46). In the heart of Jesus, prayer was endless.

It is the continuity of Jesus' prayer that the apostles and disciples understood and sought to emulate. So the apostles and the early Christians not only obeyed the command of Jesus to pray always, but tried to persevere "with him" in prayer, knowing that Jesus prayed with them.

Scholars believe, and the conscience of the church concurs, that the hourly dimension of the Liturgy of the Hours comes from Jesus' command to pray without ceasing. For instance, the Gospel accounts report that Jesus prayed at certain hours of the day. If we remember that Jesus and the apostles with the early community also prayed with the psalms, we discern that the pattern of prayer found in the Liturgy of the Hours echoes that of Christ and the early Christians.

LIMITATIONS AND POSSIBILITIES
FOR THE COUPLE'S LIFE

The prayer of the first apostolic community, cadenced over the hours of a day, preserved the tradition of the Jews—and thus the tradition of Jesus—for morning, noon, and nighttime prayer.

From the fourth century, a five-times-daily modality started to spread among Christians: *Lauds,* morning prayer; *Terce,* mid-morning prayer; *Sixt,* mid-day prayer; *None,* mid-afternoon prayer; and *Vespers,* evening prayer.[5] During the fourth century, and then more frequently in subsequent centuries, this hourly way of praying became more and more the typical prayer of monks, who live this cadence of prayer. One of the best-known versions of the Liturgy of the Hours is spelled out by Saint Benedict in his *Rule.* Benedict's version has been known and used by the church since the eighth century.

This history helps us understand the difference between time in monastic prayer and time in the prayer life of a married couple and family. While those in consecrated life suspend all their activities for prayer and conform their entire lives to this rhythm, many of the laity cannot fully practice the Liturgy of the Hours due to work and other obligations.

Despite these challenges, there are real opportunities for spouses, as a domestic church, to join the Liturgy of the Hours and the prayers of the church. I am specifically referring to the three parts many married couples already experience: Lauds, Vespers, and Compline. Some couples use them all, while others—perhaps the majority—use only one or two.

The church celebrates Lauds in the beginning of the day to remember in the new light of day the resurrection of Jesus, "the true light, which enlightens everyone" (John 1:9), and "the daybreak from on high" (Luke 1:78). Lauds lives what Psalm 5:4 suggests: "in the morning you will hear my voice; in the morning I will plead before you and wait."

We celebrate Vespers in the evening to give thanks for what was given to us during the day and for what we have done in acts of righteousness. Compline is our last prayer of the day, which we recite before going to bed, ending the day with the Lord and asking for his blessing. For those who can practice it, the Liturgy of the Hours—Lauds, Vespers, and Compline—is precious. It helps the couple to join in prayer with the church and to understand themselves as part of the body of Christ. This prayer-in-time approach can also help us to see the pain and difficulties couples encounter in their prayer lives through a liturgy of time that is connected to the places where they live.

The physical structure of the home provides the couple with domestic stations of prayer. In some, they stay in for long periods; in others, for short times. These stations regulate the day much more than schedules do, since schedules can change for many reasons.

Earlier, we looked at difficulties in organizing prayer around fixed hours of the day because work schedules, mobility, and children's needs often shift. Nevertheless, the couple needs to experience a living relationship with the Bridegroom Jesus, who is present in their lives, and of whom they are an active sacrament. These complicating factors do not exempt spouses from the need and mandate to pray always. A married couple, as much as any consecrated or single person, must rediscover Jesus constantly, seeking always to strengthen their bond with him. Spouses must consider how they can create their own hourly prayer, where they remember and seek out the Lord in friendship and companionship. The consecrated hear a bell that reminds them to pray. Married couples hear no bell, but there are other ways to construct reminders for prayer.

In the everyday life of couples and families, rhythms for prayer are suggested by the places where they live their lives. Some are places where both spouses are present; some, places of solitude; and some, places where all the family is gathered. Family members frequent them every day; in each place, we can discover the presence of the Bridegroom Jesus, and we can converse with him.

The Spouses' Bedroom

The bedroom is the sanctuary of the couple, where they can be alone together. It is the place where past and future goes. Here the intimacy of talking, as well as the giving and receiving of gestures of welcome, occur. Here, the couple's intimacy folds in upon itself, orients to infinity, and rediscovers the presence of Jesus in their shared life.

In him and for him all things have been created. He is not ashamed of the bodies he has created. He has no shame or fear of the sips the couple takes from the spring of his love. Indeed, separating the intimacy and love of marriage from Jesus is like desiring to drink clear spring water while fearing proximity to its source. With this awareness, spouses make their bedroom the first and the last place of the day where they converse with Bridegroom Jesus.

Think of the monks' prayer: praise and vespers; morning and evening; Lauds and Compline, the latter recited before bed. The bedroom is the first place spouses see when they open their eyes, and the last they see before closing them. In the bedroom, couples are called to find or invent ways of expressing the embrace with which Jesus has indissolubly linked himself to them through the sacrament of marriage. Learning how to take into account his presence, how to share with him some words in the morning and evening, means that the bedroom is no longer lived in the solitude of the couple, but in the continuous presence of Jesus.

Earlier, we described prayer as waking up from solitude; realizing that Christ is present; and then talking with him. Ours can be prayers of praise or blessing, or a spontaneous prayer; we can offer the Benedictus, the Song of Zacharias, or the *Magnificat* and add the family's own blessings and praises. We can offer normal prayers, the Our Father, Hail Mary, or Gloria Patri. It would be also beautiful if our prayers were inspired by the place, the room, or the intimacy experienced. We could offer an invocation, or thanksgiving to the Holy Spirit for the fire of his love that surpasses every form of instinct to express to our spouses a divine love.

The Dining Room

This may be the place in which we recognize the gifts and care we have received through the Lord's providence: "Look at the birds of the air: they neither sow nor reap nor gather into barns, and yet your heavenly Father feeds them. Are you not of more value than they?" (see Matthew 6:26–30 ESV). It is also the place where we can give thanks for the joy of tasting food, the gift of fellowship, and the reminder of the role the table plays in the church's larger communion. When we gather here, we have the joy of knowing that our purpose in being together in a family—even when only one parent is present—is to join with and build the big family that is our ultimate destiny.

In any home, the table is never for just one or two people. How can we determine the best size for a table in our home? Let us use the same measure as we do at the eucharistic altar. At the altar, we measure not by inches, but by our desire to have a house that will grow to embrace everyone as brothers and sisters.

Mealtimes can become moments of prayer and invocations of the Spirit designed by each couple and family. These prayers—whether at breakfast, lunch, or supper; whether all, or a few, or even one are gathered—remind us to say to ourselves and to one another, "Jesus is with us."

Thus, kitchen and dining room become the places where our hearts grow and where, in sharing, we learn to take care of others. Even when our brothers and sisters are not with us, they are in our prayers. When we pray, we remember not only those who know physical hunger, but those who hunger for something deeper. As we learn to see the dining room in this way, we also learn to pray for those in need and to share the life we have been given.

The Living Room

The living room is often just a place to watch television. We need to think of it differently. It is a place of conversation and listening, in which we learn the Word that is greater than any other words we encounter. Imagine a picture of Jesus the Teacher over the television. Such a picture offers a reference point that measures the distance between the Word and the words coming from the television. This helps us to remember to measure what we are hearing against God's Word and to know whether the words we hear are true and carry eternal life within them.

In this way, the living room becomes a room of life. Here the family grows in the awareness that this Word exists and that it needs to be accepted and heard. There we celebrate reciprocal listening: we must be able to turn off the television and give space to conversation; we must know that we are called to respond both to the Word of God and to the words of the people next to us. In this room we will learn be like Mary, the sister of Martha, who sat at Jesus' feet, listened, and gave with her heart. Sometimes we will realize that the best lines are not those on television, but those of the teacher, Jesus.

The Bathroom

The bathroom, which we frequent many times a day, can also become a place of prayer. It is the room of purification, the room of change. "Wash me thoroughly from my iniquity, and cleanse me from my sin!" (Ps. 51:2 ESV). It is the place from which we start the morning clean, on the outside and the inside. It is the place where, in the evening, we can examine our conscience and discover how our baptismal gown has been stained. We enter this room to become beautiful—combed and refreshed. There we become aware of ourselves, and we can depart from it saying, "Lord, cleanse me, wash me from all unrighteousness." The dirt on our bodies and clothing remind us that our conscience also needs to be cleaned. Our teeth need to be brushed, but our mouths need to be purified. Thus, like those in religious life attending to a ringing bell, we continue to sanctify the time in our days.

The Car

Traveling by car provides a precious time and space to dialogue with Jesus and to remember his promise: "I am with you always" (Matt. 28:20).

In our cars we can pray in many different ways: listening to the Word or to worship songs; praying alone or with the children while we take them to school; offering the rosary or prayers of praise; interceding for every person we see in other cars or on the sidewalk: "Bless him, Lord. Take care of her, Lord." It is Jesus who is in us who says: "Protect him, heavenly Father, I entrust him to you." So, why not lend our voices to Jesus?

If you travel daily by car and find yourself feeling apart from God and poor in love for those you meet, let the car be a place to refresh your heart before returning home, with the help of the Lord.

The Workplace

Here there is no ringing bell, as there is for those in religious community, to call the church to recite the Third Hour, but there is another, metaphorical bell: the working hours, a schedule, a time card to be punched. Here we can recite a prayer of invocation every time we punch a time card before working. Work can be the place where we build a new world, inside our pains, slowness, and heaviness. Work is also the place of fraternity, the environment in which the light is called to enter and lighten the darkness, to experience what Jesus lived before us: "The light shines in the darkness, and the darkness has not overcome it" (John 1:5 ESV).

How many of us at work are called, as Christians, to face a hostile environment that rejects or is offended by God? Jesus lived these moments, so we will want to live them with him too. It is a place where only the Holy Spirit can transform the situation. So why not make it a place where we invoke the Spirit, a place dedicated to constant intercessory prayer that helps us to stay in touch with Jesus? Such prayer makes visible the space that helps us to ask ourselves before people and situations: "What would Jesus do in my place? How would Jesus work in my place? How would he manage the problem I am facing?"

We could add many other places that mark our days and that would help fill our prayer time: shops, bars, places where we or our children play, movie theaters, and other amusements. If filled by prayer, all these places can help the family, the domestic church, to be in constant prayer of intercession, as Jesus, in them, is in constant prayer for his universal church.

May the Holy Spirit help us to continuously awake from our loneliness—whether individually or as a couple—and respond to Jesus, who is in our midst and who is waiting to pray with us for the church and for the whole world.

CONCLUSION

From the foundation of the world, the couple has been part of the loving project of God. In *Familiaris Consortio*, Saint John Paul II writes: "God inscribed in the humanity of man and woman the vocation, and thus the capacity and responsibility, of love and communion."[6]

The couple is that for which God has expressed his praise and wonder. From the beginning, he "found it very good" (Gen. 1:31). And in Song of Songs, the beauty between lovers becomes the paradigm for and synthesis of salvation history. It exemplifies the love of God for every person; the love of God for his people; the love of Christ for his church. Thus, marital love between spouses makes his love visible through the sacrament of marriage.

In this loving union, Jesus indissolubly bonds himself to the spouses. He becomes the Bridegroom of the couple; for them and with them he continues his loving song. In them, he continues to bless the beauty that he saw from the beginning. In them, he reveals the truth of marriage as a high expression of his love for humanity: "You have ravished my heart, my sister, my bride; you have ravished my heart with one glance of your eyes" (Song of Songs 4:9).

His great love, endless and faithful, knows no boundaries and desires to be searched for by his beloved bride; it desires to be found and permanently accepted. He wants to be loved in a way that continues in and through them his self-donating love, up to giving his life. As we read in *Familiaris Consortio*, "Spouses are therefore the permanent reminder to the Church of what happened on the Cross."[7]

Jesus rejoices when we recognize him as the Bridegroom who is present with spouses to accompany them in this nuptial dance toward the definitive marriage that is celebrated in heaven. And as the couple-bride lives in the desire and search for the Lover, for the Bridegroom with whom they share their love, they echo the Song of Songs, "I will seek him whom my soul loves" (3:2 ESV).

Thus, our unfulfilled expectations, failures of love, distance, and closed doors compel us to rush to meet the Bridegroom Jesus, as the only source of love. For he is the only one who can show us the beauty of creation within the framework of love.

This thirst for love burns in the heart of the bride who seeks the loved Bridegroom. When it finds him—when it experiences his presence—then it exalts, praises, rejoices, and multiplies in the beauty of reciprocity.

Inside this intimate meeting of the couple with Bridegroom Jesus is the mission of the spouses. As participants in the great love, they are the continuation of Jesus in the world. Together with Bridegroom Jesus, they are God's love song for each person they meet; his love song for humanity; and Jesus' love song for his bride, the church.

> *Go, O Spouses, throughout the roads of the world. Make real the Song of Songs in your everyday life, so that every person may rediscover in you God's love.*

CHAPTER STUDY OUTLINES

Chapter 1

THE LITURGY OF THE CHURCH AND THE LITURGY OF THE FAMILY

SYNOPSIS

Christian worship is a drama in two acts. These two acts do not happen one after the other, as if set in chronological order. Rather, they happen as two actions made by two actors at once and the same time. First, the church gathers giving glory, blessing, and thanksgiving to God, and as she does, her praise ascends to heaven. Second, and at the same time, God descends to earth, coming down to meet his church, to sanctify her and help her grow. At the center of the action stands Jesus Christ, who, as the protagonist of the drama, unites heaven and earth in himself in the power of the Spirit.

Every time and everywhere the church gathers, this drama is enacted. Yet, Christian worship does not begin and end at the doors of the church. It extends to the whole of life. Married couples have a unique calling and gifting to express this drama in their lives together. In the normal activities of married life, the husband and wife offer praise to God through their words and actions, and at the same time God in the Holy Spirit descends to be with them, so that they might be a sign of God's love in the world.

SCRIPTURE VERSES

Genesis 2:24–25
Ephesians 5:22–33

KEY TERMS

Liturgy: literally means "the work of the people"—generally understood to be the worship of the whole church united to Christ in the Holy Spirit where the church on earth through visible signs and actions joins with the saints and angels in heaven in offering praise and glory to God.

Sacrament: a visible sign entrusted to the church that communicates God's gift of grace; while not all streams of the church acknowledge the sacraments as such, most acknowledge that the acts of baptism and Communion are outward signs established by Jesus Christ in order to communicate God's gift of grace as it is received by faith in the life of the Christian; additionally, most would acknowledge that the acts of marriage, healing the sick, reconciliation, confirmation, and ordained ministry (i.e., the ministry of preaching the Scriptures and administering the sacraments) testify to the power of God's grace.

Marriage: the visible sign given in creation, consecrated by Christ, and entrusted to the church by which "a man shall leave his father and his mother and hold fast to his wife, and they shall become one flesh" (Gen. 2:24–25 ESV). Marriage, as a visible sign, communicates Christ's spousal love for the church. The Scriptures begin with a wedding, that of Adam and Eve, and end with a wedding, that of Christ and the church. And so, from the beginning, humanity—as male and female—has been called to embody and participate in the love of God for his bride, the church.

Domestic Church: a term used in the early church to describe the continuity between the church and the family—where the home becomes the first school of Christian life and the whole household participates in the mission of God by sharing God's love with one another and the world. From the first century to today, though in some times and places more than others, Christian households have been a family for all those who enter their doors. In the New Testament, the Greek term for household is *oikos*, where we derive our words "economy" (*oikonomia*) and "ecology" (*oikologia*). This etymological connection shows the natural connection between the household and the whole of society; we might even say that the household is the source and foundation for society both in our human interactions (*oikonomia*) and our stewardship of creation (*oikologia*).

STUDY QUESTIONS

1. Read Ephesians 5:22–33 and explain in your own words what the great mystery of marriage is.

2. How is the great mystery of marriage lived in everyday life? What are the signs of love that display and make known this mystery?

3. Reflect on your marriage or the marriages of those you know. Have you ever thought about marriage being an image and source of God's love? Can you think of any couples who exemplify this?

4. Reflect on the normal activities of your everyday life. How can these activities be a domestic liturgy where God is present to you and you are present to God?

MEMORY VERSE

"Beloved, let us love one another, for love is from God, and whoever loves has been born of God and knows God" (1 John 4:7 ESV).

RESOURCES FOR STUDY

- *Let's Start with Jesus* by Dennis Kinlaw
- *The Role of the Family in the Modern World* by John Paul II
- *Biblical and Theological Foundations of the Family: The Domestic Church* by Joseph Atkinson

Chapter 2

BAPTISM AND THE LITURGY OF THE FAMILY

SYNOPSIS

We are baptized in the name of the Father, the Son, and the Holy Spirit. This means in baptism we are given the family name and adopted into God's family. As the apostle Paul says, "In Christ Jesus you are all sons of God, through faith. For as many of you as were baptized into Christ have put on Christ" (Gal. 3:26–27 ESV). That is, through faith in Christ we are baptized into Christ and, therefore, become children of God; we become sons in the Son. What is more, in baptism we are cleansed from our sins and made ready for the wedding feast of the Eucharist. In the ancient world, a bride would take a special bath before her wedding ceremony in order to be completely cleansed from all impurity and made ready for her bridegroom. Analogously, baptism is a spiritual bath, which, by the grace of God, purifies us so that we might be united to Christ, our eternal Bridegroom.

Every married couple has received the task of growing and distributing spiritual nourishment for each person they encounter. Married couples represent the Father's love for his children. They serve as spiritual parents to all who are baptized and remind them that they are loved as children of God. Through their gestures and words married couples educate the baptized in what it means to be part of God's family.

SCRIPTURE VERSES

Romans 12:1–2
Hebrews 10:19–25

KEY TERMS

Baptism: the visible sign where we are united to Christ, washed clean by the Holy Spirit, reborn as children of God, and adopted into the family of God, the church.

Priesthood of All Believers: the calling and vocation of every baptized person to offer his or her whole life to God and live a life of holiness in the world; as the apostle Peter says, "You yourselves like living stones are being built up as a spiritual house, to be a holy priesthood, to offer spiritual sacrifices acceptable to God through Jesus Christ" (1 Peter 2:5 ESV).

Domestic Liturgy: the actions and words ("spiritual sacrifices") of everyday life that express our love for God and demonstrate the presence of Jesus in the world; the domestic liturgy of the family is the natural and spiritual extension of the eucharistic liturgy into daily life and into the heart of the world.

Domestic Trinity: the Trinity—Father, Son, and the Holy Spirit—is a communion of divine persons and a communion of love through the bond of the Holy Spirit; in an analogous way, the husband and wife are a communion of persons and a communion of love through the bond of the Holy Spirit given in marriage and baptism—in this way the husband and wife are a visible sign of Trinitarian love.

STUDY QUESTIONS

1. Read 1 Peter 2:1–10 and explain in your own words what it means to be a spiritual house.
2. Reflect on the meaning of baptism. Have you ever thought about baptism as a nuptial mystery that cleanses and prepares us for life with Jesus Christ the Bridegroom?
3. In baptism, we are made God's children and brought into his family, the church. Reflect on how the church is a family. Are there any specific ways in which you have experienced

the church as a family? Paradoxically, have you ever thought about your family being a domestic church?

4. What are the four practical suggestions for actualizing the sacrament of baptism in your domestic liturgy? Can you think of more for your own life?

MEMORY VERSE

"Like living stones, let yourselves be built into a spiritual house to be a holy priesthood to offer spiritual sacrifices acceptable to God through Jesus Christ" (1 Peter 2:5).

RESOURCES FOR STUDY

- *Jesus the Bridegroom: The Greatest Love Story Ever Told* by Brant Pitre
- *Letter to Families* by John Paul II
- *First Comes Love: Finding Your Family in the Church and in the Trinity* by Scott Hahn

Chapter 3

CONFIRMATION AND THE LITURGY OF THE FAMILY

SYNOPSIS

In the Catholic faith, as well as in several other Christian traditions, such as the Anglican and Eastern Orthodox traditions, the sacrament of confirmation imprints an indelible mark on our souls and a sacramental sign on our bodies; confirmation signifies that Jesus has marked us with the Holy Spirit and given us power to be his witnesses in the world. In confirmation, we receive an outpouring of the Holy Spirit to live a life of love and holiness like Christ; that is, we receive an outpouring of the Spirit of Christ so that we might faithfully live with the character of Christ.

For married couples, confirmation strengthens their sacramental bond so that their marriage might be filled with an indissoluble and fruitful love, flowing from the love found within the Trinity and reflecting the love between Christ and the church. The actions and words of the couple communicate this indissoluble and fruitful love to the world. In the strength of the sacrament of marriage and in the ways specific to their married life, spouses are called to make visible the gift received with confirmation. This means two basic things. First, each spouse, having been sealed by the Holy Spirit and marked with the character of Christ in confirmation, is empowered to be a witness of Christ to the other; and second, as a witness of Christ to the other, the couple together become a visible sign to the world of Christ's love for the world.

SCRIPTURE VERSES

Ezekiel 36:24–28
Galatians 4:3–7

KEY TERMS

Confirmation: the visible sign that Jesus Christ has marked us as his own and sealed us with the Holy Spirit, rooting us more deeply in our relationship with God, uniting us more firmly to Christ, increasing the gifts of the Holy Spirit in us, and making our bond with the church more perfect.

Indissoluble Love: a total, self-giving, never-surrendering, unbreakable bond of love given by the Holy Spirit to the couple in marriage so that the couple might embody the spousal love of God in the world.

Spiritual Fecundity: a calling given by God and made possible by the Holy Spirit for every man and woman, especially those who are natural fathers and mothers, to manifest the loving face of God to his children.

Theology of the Body: the recognition of the theological nature of the human body—namely that human beings do not simply *have* bodies but *are* embodied persons, whose inner life of giving and receiving love is communicated through the body as male and female—the term "theology of the body" also refers to John Paul II's reflections on the meaning of the body as made in God's image (see *Man and Woman He Created Them: A Theology of the Body* by John Paul II).

STUDY QUESTIONS

1. Read Romans 8:12–17 and explain in your own words what it means to be children of God.

2. Can you think of anyone who has been a spiritual father or mother to you or to others you know? What was the significance of that relationship?
3. What would it look like for you to be a spiritual father or mother to somebody else?
4. Reflect on the ways you communicate with your body. How do you communicate love with your body? How do you give and receive love?

MEMORY VERSE

"No one has greater love than this, to lay down one's life for one's friends" (John 15:13).

RESOURCES FOR STUDY

- *Theology of the Body for Beginners* by Christopher West
- *Man and Woman He Created Them: A Theology of the Body* by John Paul II
- *These Beautiful Bones: An Everyday Theology of the Body* by Emily Stimpson

Chapter 4

THE EUCHARIST AND THE LITURGY OF THE FAMILY

SYNOPSIS

On the night he was betrayed, Jesus instituted the Eucharist as a memorial and participation in his sacrifice on the cross for the sins of the whole world. In doing this, Jesus gave himself to his disciples so that they might have communion with him until he comes again. In a Catholic understanding of the Eucharist, Jesus entrusts himself to his beloved spouse, the church, and joins himself to her, so that the two may become one flesh. In a more general sense, all Christians proclaim that to eat the bread and drink the cup of our Lord is to proclaim the Lord's death until he comes again.

Like Jesus in the Eucharist, the family gives itself as a sacrifice for the sake of communion. The family first sacrificially gives itself to its own members, but this giving, if it is like Jesus in the Eucharist, naturally reaches out beyond itself to the church and in mission to the world. The most precious thing the family can give is the communion it has with one another, which is a gift from God and a sign of their communion with Jesus. As a "little church," the family opens itself up in generous hospitality to the world in order that the world might experience the generosity and hospitality of God. As such, the family is not a community set apart from the world but is the heart of God's mission in the world so that the world might be brought into communion with him.

SCRIPTURE VERSES

Matthew 26:26–30
John 6:22–59

KEY TERMS

Eucharist: literally means "thanksgiving"—in the Christian tradition, it refers to the visible sign instituted by Jesus Christ on the night of his betrayal, where he gave bread and wine to his disciples, instructing them to receive it as his own body and blood and commanded them to "Do this" in remembrance of him as a proclamation of his death until he comes again. Since its institution, the church has referred to this sacrament by many names—the Eucharist, Holy Communion, the Lord's Supper, the memorial of our Lord's passion and resurrection, the Holy Mass, the Blessed Sacrament, and the paschal mystery.

Permanent Sacrament: a visible sign of God's grace that extends beyond the moment of its institution and remains a sign of Christ's love in and for the world; marriage, like the Eucharist, is a permanent sacrament because the gift of God's grace and the presence of the Holy Spirit does not cease after the wedding ceremony but continues on throughout the whole life of the spouses; in fact, through the grace of the Holy Spirit, the spouses are elevated into the spousal love of Christ and the church and they are enabled to be a visible sign of God's grace to one another and those around them.

STUDY QUESTIONS

1. Read Luke 22:19 and explain in your own words what it means for Christ to give up his body.

2. Reflect on Ephesians 5:25: "Husbands, love your wives, as Christ loved the church and gave himself up for her" (ESV). How is this verse connected to Luke 22:19?

3. Reflect on the following passage: "Like the Eucharist, the family gives itself to the church and humanity as 'communion': the family 'communicates its communion.'" What is the meaning of communion? What would it look like for you to communicate communion in your daily activities?

4. Reread "The Poem of the Fount" on pages 55–56. Describe the images used by St. John of the Cross. How might the poem be an encouragement during the difficulties of family life and relationships?

MEMORY VERSE

"Jesus said to them, 'I am the bread of life; whoever comes to me will never hunger, and whoever believes in me will never thirst'" (John 6:35).

RESOURCES FOR STUDY

- *For the Life of the World: Sacraments and Orthodoxy* by Alexander Schmemann
- *On the Eucharist and Its Relationship to the Church* by John Paul II
- *Jesus and the Jewish Roots of the Eucharist: Unlocking the Secrets of the Last Supper* by Brant Pitre

Chapter 5

FORGIVENESS AND THE LITURGY OF THE FAMILY

SYNOPSIS

The sacrament of forgiveness is rooted in the person of Jesus, who experienced betrayal at the deepest level, even leading to his death. Yet, in his death Jesus gave himself to those who sinned against him. In fact, he gave himself *because* they sinned against him. What is more, in his death he gave himself for the sins of the whole world so that all who ask for forgiveness from him will find it.

If Jesus is the source and model for forgiveness, then all who receive forgiveness from him are called to forgive, as they have been forgiven. They are called to love. To ask forgiveness is to admit a failure of love. To forgive is to reconcile for the sake of love. The family is the first school of love and, therefore, the place where we learn about forgiveness; it is the place where we learn to forgive and to ask for forgiveness. As a school of love and forgiveness, the family trains us to serve as disciples of Christ's forgiveness in the world. And so we pray: "[Father,] forgive us our debts, as we also have forgiven our debtors" (Matt. 6:12 ESV).

SCRIPTURE VERSES

Psalm 130:1–8
Matthew 6:9–15

KEY TERMS

Sacrament of Forgiveness: also known as the sacrament of reconciliation and penance, is the visible sign of God's merciful pardon of our sins and offenses and the visible sign of our reconciliation with the church, who is also wounded by our sins; in this sacrament we confess our sins, turn toward Jesus in our heart and actions, and return to the Father who embraces us in his merciful love.

Community-Bride: a name for the church which, on the one hand, expresses the concrete nature of the church as a real community of people (a "little family") and, on the other hand, expresses the way in which this real community relates to Christ as a bride relates to her husband; likewise, this name for the church expresses the concrete nature of Christ's gift of himself on the cross and in the Eucharist to a real community of people and expresses the way in which Christ gives himself to this community as a husband gives himself to his bride.

STUDY QUESTIONS

1. Read Matthew 26:14–25. What do you think it was like for Jesus to share this meal with the one who would betray him that very night? Read Matthew 26:26–35. What do you think it was like for Jesus to share this meal with the one who would deny him three times that very night?

2. Reflect on the depths of Jesus' love for Judas and Peter. What does it mean for Jesus to give himself to those who betray him and deny him? What does it mean for him to give himself *because* of such betrayal and denial?

3. How do Judas and Peter respond to Jesus' love for them? (See Matthew 27:3–10 and John 21:1–23.) How do you respond to Jesus' love for you?

4. Have you ever denied or betrayed someone? Have you ever been denied or betrayed by someone? How might Jesus be a source and model for forgiveness and reconciliation in these relationships? What would it look like for the liturgy of the family to be a place for forgiveness and reconciliation?

MEMORY VERSE

"If we confess our sins, he who is faithful and just will forgive us our sins and cleanse us from all unrighteousness" (1 John 1:9 ESV).

RESOURCES FOR STUDY

*   *Living Love: A Modern Edition of Treatise on the Love of God* by Francis de Sales
*   *Reconciliation and Penance in the Mission of the Church Today* by John Paul II
*   *Love Alone Is Credible* by Hans Urs von Balthasar

Chapter 6

THE ANOINTING OF THE SICK AND THE LITURGY OF THE FAMILY

SYNOPSIS

In the anointing of the sick, Jesus cares for those who suffer in their bodies. By his death and resurrection, Jesus not only heals our sins and diseases, but redeems our bodies so that in the life to come we will have resurrected bodies which will not be subject to sickness and death. What is more, in his death and resurrection, Jesus gives us the hope of new meaning to the suffering we experience in this life. In him our suffering can be transfigured into sanctification and even union with God. When we suffer in illness or death, we are united to Christ and, in a sense, participate in his redemptive passion and death; thus, our bodily tribulations are an opportunity to make a living sacrifice to God and contribute to the good of the people of God.

As a conduit of Christ's healing presence in the world, the family is called to pray for healing, care for the sick, comfort the suffering, and give rest to the weary. Since the church is the family of God and the family is the domestic church, the family has the unique opportunity to serve as an icon of the family of God as she cares for the sick, who at times have little or no family to care for them. What is more, the family prepares those at death's door for their passage into the presence of their eternal and heavenly Father and their entrance into the communion of saints in heaven, who are our spiritual brothers and sisters. Finally, married couples uniquely remind the sick and dying of the eternal hope and joy found beyond the grave in the wedding feast of the Lamb. As married couples tend for one another and together tend for others, they "weep with those who weep" and at the same time make ready the bride for the day when the Bridegroom will wipe away her tears and death will be no more.

SCRIPTURE VERSES

Psalm 30:1–12
James 5:13–16

KEY TERMS

Sacrament of Anointing: also known as the sacrament of healing, the visible sign of God's grace and care for the sick where the church commends the sick to God by anointing them with oil and praying for their healing, both spiritually and physically, and exhorts the sick to freely unite themselves to Christ in his suffering for them on the cross.

Priests of Life: the priestly call of spouses to be present to one another and their children at every stage of life from birth to death—thus revealing that we cannot truly care for the sick if we are not attentive to life at every other point of its development.

Gospel of Life: the good news and celebration of life at every stage from conception to natural death—where every human life has a supernatural value and dignity because it is a gift from God, made in the image of God, and called to communion with God.

STUDY QUESTIONS

1. What is the first grace of the sacrament of anointing the sick? What is the purpose of this first grace and how does it heal us?
2. What is the new meaning given to suffering by Christ's own suffering and death? Compare this new meaning of suffering

with other ways of understanding suffering, particularly with the modern focus on health.

3. Reflect on a time when you or someone close to you experienced a time of suffering. How might that experience of suffering been a participation in the suffering of Christ and a contribution to the good of the people of God?

4. What unique gift can a spouse bring to another when one of them is suffering? What gift can they bring together to others who are suffering?

MEMORY VERSE

"Rejoice insofar as you are sharing Christ's sufferings, so that you may also be glad and shout for joy when his glory is revealed" (1 Peter 4:13 NRSV).

RESOURCES FOR STUDY

- *The Problem of Pain* by C. S. Lewis
- *The Gospel of Life* by John Paul II
- *Holy Eros: A Liturgical Theology of the Body* by Adam Cooper

Chapter 7

THE LITURGY OF THE WORD IN THE FAMILY

SYNOPSIS

The Word of God is God's personal voice and address to us. It invites us to respond to him and live in communion with him. The "Word of God" has a twofold meaning. First and chiefly, the Word is Jesus Christ, who is the Word made flesh. Second and sacramentally, the Word is sacred Scripture, given by God and received by his people, the church. As such, the Word of God is not essentially a book on a shelf but a Person. Yet, in order to know this Person, Jesus Christ, we must immerse ourselves in the Word, as Scripture. Otherwise we risk living with Christ without knowing who he really is.

Jesus Christ, as God's Word, communicated God's love for the world through his words and actions, most of all through the gift of himself on the cross. Analogously, spouses are called to communicate Christ's self-giving love for the world in their love for one another. This is only possible if the spouses know Christ as he has revealed himself through sacred Scripture. Therefore, spouses must have a deep knowledge of Scripture and make it part of the liturgy of the family.

SCRIPTURE VERSES

Deuteronomy 11:18–21
John 1:1–18

KEY TERMS

Nuptial Dialogue: the Word spoken to man from God in creation, through Scripture, and most especially in Jesus Christ, who is the Word of God made flesh and the visible sign of God's spousal love for the world; conversely, it is also man's response to God's Word.

Sacramentality of the Word of God: in the mystery of the incarnation, the eternal Word of God became flesh and made visible, through human words and actions, that which is invisible, namely God himself; in this way, Jesus Christ became the visible sign of God's Word in the world, and it is he who is present and speaking through the Word of God in Scripture.

Home of the Word: the church is the familial context—the home—within which God speaks his Word to the world, and the liturgy is the privileged setting within which God speaks to his family and his family responds back to him in prayer and praise.

STUDY QUESTIONS

1. Have you ever thought about sacred Scripture being the voice of Jesus the Bridegroom speaking to you, his bride?
2. Do you know any older married couples whose relationship embodies the eternal youth of marriage? How is their relationship a wedding portrait of the eternal and timeless love of Christ for the church?
3. Read Colossians 3:12–17. In your own words explain what it means to "let the word of Christ dwell in you richly." What would it look like for Christ the Bridegroom to dwell in your heart?
4. Reflect on the following statement: "The Bible is the concrete way through which the Bridegroom Jesus can speak in a home and be a living and active protagonist in the family." List the ways in which the Bible can be part of your daily life and the liturgy of the family.

MEMORY VERSE

"Your word is a lamp to my feet and a light to my path" (Ps. 119:105 ᴇsᴠ).

RESOURCES FOR STUDY

- *The Bible and the Liturgy* by Jean Danielou
- *Consuming the Word: The New Testament and the Eucharist in the Early Church* by Scott Hahn
- *Sanctified Vision: An Introduction to Early Christian Interpretation of the Bible* by John J. O'Keefe and R. R. Reno

Chapter 8

THE LITURGY OF THE HOURS IN THE FAMILY

SYNOPSIS

Prayer is our response to God. If God has spoken to us in his Word, then prayer is our response to that Word. Prayer is a personal articulation of love and an awakening from our loneliness and self-isolation toward a life of relationship with God. In prayer, we open ourselves up to God and give ourselves to him. The Liturgy of the Hours provides a rhythm of prayer for all Christians who desire to pray without ceasing and carry on a nuptial dialogue with the Lord throughout the day.

Though the everyday life of the family is filled with busy schedules and different events, our daily routines can actually provide a liturgy of the hours for us. Our daily routines take us to certain places every day and these places can serve as stations of prayer throughout our day. These stations can serve as opportunities to pray whether alone, with a spouse, or with the whole family. Like the Liturgy of the Hours, our stations mark our day, and like the ringing of the monastery bell, they remind us to turn our attention to God in prayer, even if for a moment.

SCRIPTURE VERSES

Psalm 34:1–10
Matthew 6:5–15

KEY TERMS

Liturgy of the Hours: also known as the Breviary or Divine Office, a pattern of daily prayer originating from the liturgical worship of the Jewish temple, the example and commands Jesus, and the practices of the early church; currently practiced by priests, monks, nuns, and laity around the world so that the church may pray without ceasing and sanctify the hours and minutes of each and every day.

Stations of Prayer: the places which regulate our daily routines and activities and give us the opportunity to pray wherever we go (e.g., the bedroom, dining room, living room, bathroom, transport, and workplace) and thus discover the presence of Jesus the Bridegroom throughout the day.

STUDY QUESTIONS

1. Reflect on the following passage: "There is always someone who preceded me. As a mother precedes a child, as a mother begets a child, so God has always wanted me to exist and never forgets me." What is the significance of someone who always preceded us? Can anybody account for his or her own existence? If not, then is life always a response to God's prior desire and love for us?

2. Reflect on the relationship between the Liturgy of the Word and the Liturgy of the Hours. If the Word of God is God speaking to us, then in what way is prayer our response back to God? What does this say about the nuptial dialogue between Christ the Bridegroom and the church, his bride?

3. Laity and married couples do not have a monastery bell calling them to pray the Liturgy of the Hours, but this does not mean they are not called to pray. What other ways—other "bells"—can remind them to pray throughout the day?

4. Reflect on the stations of prayer in your daily and weekly routine. How can these stations become a place of encountering the presence of Jesus the Bridegroom?

MEMORY VERSE

"Rejoice always, pray without ceasing, give thanks in all circumstances; for this is the will of God in Christ Jesus for you" (1 Thess. 5:16–18 ESV).

RESOURCES FOR STUDY

- *The School of Prayer: An Introduction to the Divine Office for All Christians* by John Brook
- *Psalms and Canticles: Meditations and Catechesis on the Psalms and Canticles of Morning Prayer* by John Paul II
- *Prayer* by Hans Urs von Balthasar

NOTES

Chapter 1

1. *Catechism of the Catholic Church*, 2nd ed. (Washington, DC: United States Catholic Conference, 2011), sec. 1088, www .usccb.org/beliefs-and-teachings/what-we-believe/catechism /catechism-of-the-catholic-church/epub/index.cfm.
2. Ibid., sec. 1084.
3. Ibid., sec. 1086.
4. Ibid., sec. 1089.
5. Ibid., sec. 1104.
6. Ibid., sec. 1113.
7. Ibid., sec. 1131.
8. John Paul II, *Familiaris Consortio* [On the Role of the Christian Family in the Modern World], November 22, 1981, sec. 56, w2.vatican.va/content/john-paul-ii/en/apost _exhortations/documents/hf_jp-ii_exh_19811122 _familiaris-consortio.html.
9. The ministerial priesthood (i.e., the one of the priests) serves the baptismal priesthood. There is no dignity in the world higher than being a child of God and being a part of the body of Jesus. Therefore, a ministerial priest is never

above the others, but rather *under* the others, to serve a community of God. The ministries of deacons, priests, bishops, and the pope add nothing to the dignity of being a child of God, because this is already the highest possible attainment. A ministerial priest descends to clean the feet of the community so that the community can offer sacrifices of praise with pure hearts.

10. John Paul II, *Familiaris Consortio,* sec. 13.
11. See Genesis 1:31. According to recent studies on the Greek version of the Bible, *beautiful,* rather than *good,* is the adjective best suited to describe the pleasure of God.
12. John Paul II, *Familiaris Consortio,* sec. 56.
13. Catholic Church, *The Rite of Marriage: the Roman Ritual revised by decree of the Second Vatican Ecumenical Council and published by the authority of Pope Paul VI* (New York: Alba House, 1997).
14. Ibid., *Praenotanda,* 11.
15. Achille M. Triacca, *Matrimonio e verginità: Teologia e celebrazione per una pienezza di vita in Cristo* (Vatican City: Libraria Editrice Vaticana, 2005), 250.
16. John Paul II, *Familiaris Consortio,* sec. 13.
17. Robert Bellarmine, S.J., *De controversiis,* t. III, *De matr,* controvers. II, cap. 6.
18. Paul VI, *Gaudium et Spes* [The Pastoral Constitution on the church in the Modern World], December 7, 1965, sec. 48, www.vatican.va/archive/hist_councils/ii_vatican_council /documents/vat-ii_cons_19651207_gaudium-et-spes_en.html.
19. Triacca, *Matrimonio e verginità,* 251.
20. Ibid.
21. "Evangelism and Marriage," a pastoral document of the Italian Episcopal Conference.

Chapter 2

1. Robert Bellarmine, S.J., *De controversiis,* t. III, *De matr,* controvers. II, cap. 6.
2. Cf. John Paul II, *Familiaris Consortio,* [On the Role of the Christian Family in the Modern World], November 22, 1981,

sec. 13: "Like each of the seven sacraments, so also marriage is a real symbol of the event of salvation, but in its own way. The spouses participate in it as spouses, together, as a couple, so that the first and immediate effect of marriage (*res et sacramentum*) is not supernatural grace itself, but the Christian conjugal bond, a typically Christian communion of two persons because it represents the mystery of Christ's incarnation and the mystery of His covenant. The content of participation in Christ's life is also specific: conjugal love involves a totality, in which all the elements of the person enter—appeal of the body and instinct, power of feeling and affectivity, aspiration of the spirit and of will. It aims at a deeply personal unity, the unity that, beyond union in one flesh, leads to forming one heart and soul; it demands indissolubility and faithfulness in definitive mutual giving; and it is open to fertility (cf. Paul VI, *Humanae vitae*, sec. 9). In a word, it is a question of the normal characteristics of all natural conjugal love, but with a new significance which not only purifies and strengthens them, but raises them to the extent of making them the expression of specifically Christian values."

3. John Paul II, *Familiaris Consortio*, sec. 56.
4. *Catechism of the Catholic Church,* 2nd ed. (Washington, DC: United States Catholic Conference, 2011), sec. 1617.
5. John Paul II, *Familiaris Consortio*, sec. 13.
6. "Since all Christians have become by rebirth of water and the Holy Spirit a new creature so that they should be called and should be children of God, they have a right to a Christian education." Paul VI, *Gravissimum educationis* [Declaration on Christian Education], sec. 2, October 28, 1965, www.vatican.va/archive/hist_councils/ii_vatican_council/documents/vat-ii_decl_19651028_gravissimum-educationis_en.html.
7. John Paul II, *Familiaris Consortio*, sec. 13.
8. Second Vatican Council, *Lumen gentium* [Dogmatic Constitution on the church], November 21, 1964, sec. 10, www.vatican.va/archive/hist_councils/ii_vatican_council/documents/vat-ii_const_19641121_lumen-gentium_en.html.

Chapter 3

1. *Catechism of the Catholic Church*, 2nd ed. (Washington, DC: United States Catholic Conference, 2011), sec. 1303, www.usccb.org/beliefs-and-teachings/what-we-believe /catechism/catechism-of-the-catholic-church/epub /index.cfm.

2. *Code of Canon Law*, c. 1065 §1, in *The Code of Canon Law* (Vatican City: Vatican, 1983). Retrieved from www.vatican .va/archive/ENG1104/__P3W.HTM.

3. *Catechism*, sec. 1304.

4. Ibid., sec. 1302.

5. Ibid, sec. 1303; Second Vatican Council, *Lumen gentium* [Dogmatic Constitution on the church], November 21, 1964, sec. 11, www.vatican.va/archive/hist_councils/ii_vatican _council/documents/vat-ii_const_19641121_lumen-gentium _en.html.

6. *Catechism*, sec. 1303.

7. John Paul II, *Grattisimam sane* [Letter to Families], sec. 6, February 2, 1994, w2.vatican.va/content/john-paul-ii/en /letters/1994/documents/hf_jp-ii_let_02021994_families .html.

8. Benedict XVI, *Deus Caritas Est* [On Christian Love] sec. 2, December 25, 2005, w2.vatican.va/content/benedict-xvi/en /encyclicals/documents/hf_ben-xvi_enc_20051225_deus -caritas-est.html.

9. *Catechism*, sec. 1303.

10. Ibid., sec. 1304.

Chapter 4

1. *Catechism of the Catholic Church*, 2nd ed. (Washington, DC: United States Catholic Conference, 2011), sec. 1323, www .usccb.org/beliefs-and-teachings/what-we-believe /catechism/catechism-of-the-catholic-church/epub /index.cfm.

2. John Paul II, *Familiaris Consortio* [On the Role of the Christian Family in the Modern World], November 22, 1981, sec. 19, w2.vatican.va/content/john-paul-ii/en/apost _exhortations/documents/hf_jp-ii_exh_19811122_familiaris -consortio.html.

3. Ibid., sec. 13.

4. Ibid.

5. Ibid., sec. 20.

6. *Catechism*, sec. 1404.

7. John Paul II, *Familiaris Consortio*, sec. 38.

8. Ibid., sec. 12.

9. 1 Peter 2:5; *Familiaris Consortio*, sec. 59.

10. John Paul II, *Familiaris Consortio*, sec. 18.

11. Ibid., sec. 17.

12. John of the Cross, trans. Kieran Kavanaugy and Otilio Rodriguez, *The Collected Work of Saint John of the Cross* (Washington, DC: ICS Publications, 1991), n.p.

Chapter 5

1. John Paul II, *Familiaris Consortio* [On the Role of the Christian Family in the Modern World], November 22, 1981, sec. 13, w2.vatican.va/content/john-paul-ii/en /apost_exhortations/documents/hf_jp-ii_exh_19811122 _familiaris-consortio.html.

2. See www.saintaquinas.com/prayers.html.

3. Ibid.

4. John Paul II, *Familiaris Consortio*, sec. 13.

Chapter 6

1. *Catechism of the Catholic Church*, 2nd ed. (Washington, DC: United States Catholic Conference, 2011), sec. 1512, www. usccb.org/beliefs-and-teachings/what-we-believe /catechism/catechism-of-the-catholic-church/epub /index.cfm.

2. Second Vatican Council, *Lumen gentium* [Dogmatic Constitution on the church], November 21, 1964, sec. 11, www.vatican.va/archive/hist_councils/ii_vatican_council /documents/vat-ii_const_19641121_lumen-gentium _en.html.
3. *Catechism*, sec. 1503.
4. Ibid., 1504.
5. Ibid., 1505.
6. Ibid.
7. Ibid., 1506.
8. Ibid., 1507.
9. Ibid., 1508.
10. Ibid.; see Colossians 1:24.
11. *Catechism*, sec. 1509.
12. Ibid., 1520.
13. Ibid.
14. Ibid., 1521.
15. *Lumen gentium*, sec. 11.
16. *Catechism*, sec 1522.
17. Ibid., 1523.
18. Paul VI, *Gaudium et Spes* [The Pastoral Constitution on the church in the Modern World], December 7, 1965, sec. 49, www.vatican.va/archive/hist_councils/ii_vatican_council /documents/vat-ii_cons_19651207_gaudium-et-spes_en.html.
19. John Paul II, *Evangelium Vitae* [On the Value and Inviolability of Human Life], sec. 83, March 25, 1995, w2.vatican.va/ content/john-paul-ii/en/encyclicals/documents /hf_jp-ii_enc_25031995_evangelium-vitae.html.
20. "*Cupio dissolvi et esse cum Christo*"; see Philippians 1:23.

Chapter 7

1. See Matthew 28:20; Pope Benedict XVI, *Verbum Domini* [On the Word of God in the Life and Mission of the Church], sec. 51, September 30, 2010, w2.vatican.va/content/benedict

-xvi/en/apost_exhortations/documents/hf_ben-xvi_exh
_20100930_verbum-domini.html.

2. See Colossians 3:16; Second Vatican Council, *Dei Verbum*
   [Dogmatic Constitution on Divine Revelation], November 18,
   1965, sec. 8, www.vatican.va/archive/hist_councils/ii
   _vatican_council/documents/
   vat-ii_const_19651118_dei-verbum_en.html.

3. See Colossians 1:15; 1 Timothy 1:17; Exodus 33:11; John
   15:14–15; Baruch 3:38; *Dei Verbum*, sec. 2.

4. See Hebrews 1:1–2; John 1:1–18, 3:34, 5:36, 17:4; *Dei Verbum*,
   sec. 4.

5. See John 1:14; "The reality of the revealed mystery is offered
   to us in the 'flesh' of the Son," *Verbum Domini*, sec. 56.

6. *Verbum Domini*, sec. 52.

7. Second Vatican Council, *Sacrosanctum Concilium*
   [Constitution on the Sacred Liturgy], ch. III, sec. 24,
   December 4, 1963, www.vatican.va/archive/hist_councils
   /ii_vatican_council/documents/vat-ii_const_19631204
   _sacrosanctum-concilium_en.html.

8. *Sacrosanctum Concilium*, ch. I, sec. 7; *Verbum Domini*, sec. 52.

9. *Verbum Domini*, sec. 52.

10. Ibid., sec. 85.

11. Paul VI, *Gaudium et Spes* [The Pastoral Constitution on the
    church in the Modern World], December 7, 1965, sec. 48,
    www.vatican.va/archive/hist_councils/ii_vatican_council
    /documents/vat-ii_cons_19651207_gaudium-et-spes_en.html.

12. See Matthew 25:24–26; Luke 15:8–9; Song of Songs 4:12.

13. *Dei Verbum*, sec. 25.

14. *Sacrosanctum Concilium*, ch. I, sec. 7.

15. Family Communities for Evangelization are small commu-
    nities of believers led by a married couple who gather to
    share prayer, the Word, and the faith. They are present in
    the United States with the name of Amore Communities
    and in Italy in several dioceses.

16. Renzo Bonetti, *Felici e Santi: La Vita Interiore degli Sposi* (Rome:
    Paoline, 2011), n. p.

17. Ambrose, *De Officiis Ministrorum*, I, 20, 88, retrieved from www.newadvent.org/fathers/34011.htm; *Dei Verbum*, sec. 25.

Chapter 8

1. *Catechism of the Catholic Church*, 2nd ed. (Washington, DC: United States Catholic Conference, 2011), sec. 2560, www.usccb.org/beliefs-and-teachings/what-we-believe/cate-chism/catechism-of-the-catholic-church/epub/index.cfm.
2. See http://www.vatican.va/archive/hist_councils/ii_vatican_council/documents/vat-ii_const_19631204_sacrosanctum-concilium_en.html.
3. *General Instructions for the Liturgy of the Hours*, ch. I–III, sec. 10. www.catholicliturgy.com/index.cfm/FuseAction/DocumentContents/Index/2/SubIndex/39/DocumentIndex/2.
4. *General Instructions*, ch. I–I, sec. 4.
5. As recalled by Tertullian, "On Prayer, 25," (public domain).
6. John Paul II, *Familiaris Consortio* [On the Role of the Christian Family in the Modern World], November 22, 1981, sec. 11, w2.vatican.va/content/john-paul-ii/en/apost_exhortations/documents/hf_jp-ii_exh_19811122_familiaris-consortio.html.
7. Ibid., sec. 13.